Growing into your future . . .
requires a dedication to caring for yourself
as if you were rare and precious,
which you are, and regarding all life
around you as equally so,
which it is.

VICTORIA MORAN

SELF-LOVE
through the
Sacred
FEMININE

A Guide through the Paintings & Channelings of **Jo Jayson**

REDFeather™

MIND | BODY | SPIRIT

Printed in China

Other Schiffer Books on Related Subjects:

AboraMana: Channeled Goddess Wisdom Cards, Neithard Horn,
ISBN: 978-0-7643-3696-6

Gaian Tarot: Healing the Earth, Healing Ourselves, Joanna Powell Colbert,
ISBN: 978-0-7643-5062-7

Cover design by Justin Watkinson
Designed by Brenda McCallum

Type set in Bickham Script/ Minion

ISBN: 978-0-7643-5718-3
Printed in China

Published by Red Feather Mind, Body, Spirit
An imprint of Schiffer Publishing, Ltd.
4880 Lower Valley Road
Atglen, PA 19310
Phone: (610) 593-1777; Fax: (610) 593-2002
E-mail: Info@schifferbooks.com
Web: www.redfeathermbs.com

For our complete selection of fine books on this and related subjects, please visit our website at www.schifferbooks.com. You may also write for a free catalog.

Schiffer Publishing's titles are available at special discounts for bulk purchases for sales promotions or premiums. Special editions, including personalized covers, corporate imprints, and excerpts, can be created in large quantities for special needs. For more information, contact the publisher.

We are always looking for people to write books on new and related subjects. If you have an idea for a book, please contact us at
proposals@schifferbooks.com.

To my children, Daniel and Daisy,
for being with me on this journey back towards self-love.
Thank you for your unwavering and continued love and patient
support, and for being my guides and helpers in the birth of these
thirteen paintings in my studio over the past years.

A special thanks goes to all the people who were chosen
to be models for these paintings. Looking back, I didn't choose any
of you; you all came into my life with incredible synchronicity and
perfection, but all of you were chosen by my guides to hold the
energy of that which wanted to be expressed. I was shown an image,
and you helped me re-create it. I did not use models for all the
paintings, but for those that I did, thank you for your
generosity and service to this work.

Contents

A NOTE FROM THE ARTIST AND AUTHOR
7

FOREWORD
by Gail Swanson
13

INTRODUCTION
15

CHAPTER 1   GUINEVERE: THE QUEEN
Self-Love, Self-Honor, and Self-Respect
21

CHAPTER 2   MARIAMNE OF MAGDALA: THE MAGDALENE
Embracing the Sacred Feminine within Yourself
31

CHAPTER 3   BRIGHID: MOTHER GODDESS OF IRELAND
Flowing with the Cycles and Changes of Life and Womanhood
41

CHAPTER 4   ISIS: ONE WHO IS ALL
Internal Power, Empowerment, and Taking Your Power Back
51

CHAPTER 5   MARY: THE MOTHER
Comfort and Support, Asking for Help, Self-Talk
61

CHAPTER 6 JEANNE D'ARC: MAID OF ORLÉANS
Finding Faith, Courage, and Strength
71

CHAPTER 7 MIRIAM: THE PROPHETESS
Choosing Hope and Finding Joy
81

CHAPTER 8 GUAN YIN: MOTHER OF COMPASSION
AND MERCY
Compassion and Forgiveness for Others and the Self
91

CHAPTER 9 MORGAN LE FEY: THE WATER SPIRIT
Embracing the Light and Dark in Our Lives
103

CHAPTER 10 ARTEMIS: MAIDEN OF THE HUNT
Independence, Boundaries, and Focused Intention
113

CHAPTER 11 KALI MA: THE DARK MOTHER
Endings, Beginnings, Allowing for Change
123

CHAPTER 12 INANNA: STAR OF HEAVEN AND EARTH
Disrobing of the False Self and Embracing Your Sexuality and Sensuality
131

CHAPTER 13 GRANDMOTHER SPIDER: THE WEAVER
Becoming the Wise Woman, Weaving the Web of Your Own Life
143

IN CONCLUSION . . .
150

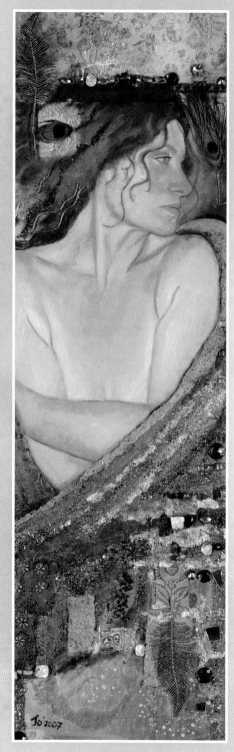

Deep Waters Self Portrait, 2006.

A Note from the Artist and Author

Most of us, at some point in our lives, are faced with emotional turmoil. Our lives may be turned upside down by illness, death, divorce, or loss. We may feel lost at sea, alone and fearfully facing the unknown.

Depending on our personal journey, this life-changing whirlwind we find ourselves in may offer us an opportunity to look in the mirror. Our reflection is often an unwelcome and uncomfortable witnessing of our "self" crying out for help and asking us to heal and grow.

The journey of self-healing has many paths; the path outlined in this book is just *one* way. It is the path I was led on by my soul's guidance and the encouragement of Spirit.

After a very painful divorce, I was left feeling lost, scared, and alone, which forced me to become acutely aware of my relationships, weaknesses, strengths, and the inner workings of my true self. Forging a new beginning takes courage, of which I thought I had a limited supply. I was paralyzed with fear: fear of being alone, of being unlovable, of failure and success, of never being able to be an artist again, and of never being self-sufficient. I was afraid to love again. I was also in the midst of a chronic disease, leaving me in puddles of tears, pain, and panic nearly every day and night.

About the time my marriage ended, I was already in the middle of my first series of paintings, called the "Goddess Chakra Series." I used chakra healing to help rebalance myself and gain some stability during the breakdown of my marriage and family. As I painted these images, I sensed I was experiencing something I had never experienced before as an artist. Information about the chakra system came to me that I had never read in a book, nor learnt in a class; there was no tangible source for it. As I created these paintings, I was guided to bring forth a special vibration to each of them. Indeed, I found myself painting in a way I never had before. It was then I began to realize that I might be channeling the paintings.

After I completed the series and brought out the meditation kit, I started teaching chakra healing workshops and seminars. As I spoke and taught, information continued to flow to me in a profound knowing—one that was so cloaked in the truth that I never doubted it.

In 2011, I unveiled the first of the Sacred Feminine series: *Guinevere the Queen*. Guinevere was an energy I had known and understood since I was a child. Drawn as deeply to the myths and legends of Arthurian times as I was, Guinevere felt familiar and close.

It was at this point I knew that something more than just painting a beautiful image was happening. I was truly being guided by something bigger than my own imagination. I started to receive information about Guinevere and her message to the world, especially to women. I was clearly told that I needed to paint another twelve images. Together with Guinevere, this would become the series called "Expressions of the Sacred Feminine."

The next painting was *Mariamne of Magdala, The Magdalene*. She took two long, difficult months to paint. As I worked, I noticed I was being put through an agonizing test in compassion for others and the self. This painting became such a success via social media that the responses I received were beyond anything I could have imagined. It touched people in ways I had never believed possible. By the time I got to the fourth painting, of Isis, I had been pushed and pulled through so many tests and challenges and given such interesting wisdom attached to each one, I had no doubt that the information was directly from Spirit. It came to me for my own healing, but more importantly, I was also being pushed to share these messages with others.

On March 28, 2016, I finished the thirteenth and last painting of the series, *Grandmother Spider*. Over the past several years, I had gathered and compiled all the information about each of the thirteen Sacred Feminine archetypes and collected all the wisdom and messages that flowed through me whilst carrying their energies.

It wasn't until I had painted the seventh feminine energy in the series that I realized why there were only going to be thirteen. Thirteen is a sacred number, one that is held most holy in the Kabbalah; it is believed to hold the energy of the Divine Feminine or *Shekinah* (Hebrew for feminine face of God) within it. I have often been asked why I painted *these* specific thirteen energies and not any of the hundreds of other Goddess archetypes out there. The truth is that I don't know the whole answer; I have no idea why these specific feminine energies came to me in this particular order. Initially, I thought perhaps it was a lineage I was expressing, but in time I realized these were the energies and archetypes my *soul* was familiar with from over many lifetimes, even though I wasn't familiar with them in my current life as Jo Jayson. Interestingly, some of these feminine energies had once been incarnated and lived here on earth, but others were celestial energies who were completely non-corporeal.

I believe that human consciousness and the human psyche create physical expressions of that which it subconsciously remembers in spirit. For energies such as Artemis, Isis, and Grandmother Spider, the memory in our cells and souls acts as a catalyst to create names, identities, and expressions of each vibration of a Divine aspect we subconsciously remember. This is why many Goddess archetypes are repeated and reflected in varying guises in different cultures around the globe.

Some people have asked what the purpose of the "Sacred Feminine Series" is. I believe I was given energies to paint the Goddesses who represent aspects of *ALL* of us; that is why this series of paintings has been so beautifully received and so many are drawn to it. We recognize ourselves in these feminine archetypes, not merely physically, but in their wisdom and message, either because we recognize the lesson as one we chose to work on in this lifetime or because we ourselves embody that same lesson. Some we recognize immediately, finding ourselves magnetically attracted to a particular archetype or energy; others become familiar to us at different times in our lives as our psyche changes and evolves. I believe all of these energies—whether formerly physical beings who have walked this earth, or those who have always remained in the celestial dimensions—came to me not only to be physically expressed, but to have their message reflected and shared. The thirteen Sacred Feminine energies I have painted are bright beacons of light for us. They are masters, teachers, guides, and spiritual friends. They ask neither to be worshipped nor that we feel separate from them; they only ask that we recognize them within ourselves. After all, are we not all one? Are we not all aspects of the Divine?

I have also been asked about the process of painting these images. I paint very realistically and I use models. For some of the feminine energies, I used composite images of models that, when put together, created what I was clearly being shown. For many others, I was literally *given* the physical model and shown the pose. Those who were chosen to be the models for some of these paintings will understand this statement very clearly. The magical synchronicity of these women suddenly appearing in my life for the sole purpose of being the model, and subsequently the vessel, that would hold the energy for that particular Sacred Feminine being has been one of the most joyous and blessed experiences in this whole process. Spirit knew I needed models to paint; over the past six years of this journey, I have never had to go looking for a model. Before each new painting was created, the perfect person simply arrived. So many magical events surrounded my models, too many to describe; however, I will say that, without any doubt, these models were chosen by the thirteen feminine energies themselves, and the process in the unveiling of that has been one of the most magical in this entire journey.

In 2016, I taught a seven-week online course based on the paintings and channeling called *Self-Love through the Sacred Feminine.* I laid out the path I had been shown and walked, and received beautiful testimonial confirmations for the help and inspiration this work provided my students.

It has been a long, arduous journey on this path back towards self-love, and each wobbly step along the way I have been held in unconditional love by my connection to Spirit. Learning to love yourself unconditionally and heal all wounds from the past is a brave endeavor; without my faith, I am not sure I would have made it.

It is this path that I now lay out in this book for you. As with all things, the more you put of yourself into something, the more your "self" receives back. This book can be read through once, or it can be poured over, going back and forth and delving into each chapter time and time again until the lesson fully resonates with every part of you.

Call of The Nightingale, 2011.

Foreword

BY

GAIL SWANSON

The Divine Feminine is a Sisterhood, which is now breaking the chains of bondage that have held her for so long.

Sisters are supporting and encouraging one another. This Sisterhood is a power and a force like no other. We work individually *and* collectively; the intent is the same. It is ancient, pure, and sanctified. It is a power that will change the world.

The Divine Feminine has been awakening us one by one. Together, we are merging and forming a new way of being, unshackled and free.

Every woman is a channel for the Divine Feminine. Some are meant to be more public in their mission to express their particular spark of her, but every woman channels her just the same.

Each time you speak up, each time you step out of where you are comfortable and sing, dance, paint, create, you are sending out and magnifying her vibration on earth and beyond. Feel what the Divine Feminine means to you.

Perhaps when you do not feel you have the strength to overcome something, and yet you *do,* this is the Divine Feminine, that majesty, aiding in all you do and all you are.

I have been aware of and inspired by Jo Jayson's Divine Feminine Awakening for many years. When the Divine Feminine came calling, Jo answered, and Goddess after Goddess spoke through her in words and through the magic of her brush upon the canvas.

When the call comes, you *must* answer, because this is what is creating a new world—a world of infinite possibility, infinite creation, and infinite wisdom.

In reading *Self-Love through the Sacred Feminine*, I found the journey through the book to be a loving demonstration of who we are and where we are going. Jo reveals her own struggles along the way, and one way or another, these are the struggles of us all.

There are practical prayers and meditations given for what each Goddess has brought forth; each Goddess in the book comes forward to give us her own pearls of wisdom, to allow us to remember that all we need has always been within. We are given a spiritual guidepost to help us navigate through sometimes very difficult passages as women on the path of Awakening. As we move through each Goddess we are reminded again and again that as we begin to love ourselves, we will truly remember our own Goddess within.

Jo and I have had very similar paths through the magic and trials of our own spiritual Awakening. We both struggle with a chronic illness, and both of us have experienced a major spiritual Awakening alongside our physical challenges.

This is where the Divine Feminine Partnership comes in. This is where your *will* comes in.

Will you accept your mission to allow the power of the Divine Feminine to flow through you no matter the sacrifice? If you say yes, as Jo has done, and persevere no matter what, you will crack the shell of illusion that has held us all for so long, and the sweetest song you have ever heard will be born. When your own Divine Feminine begins to awaken many times through some very dark nights of the soul, it can also awaken within a spark of all the Divine Feminine throughout all time and space. When this power begins to move through you, you have a choice to resist or to allow the energy to take you on a journey that is meant not only for you, but for the many. It is not for the faint of heart.

Through her own loving and courageous heart and the energy of all the Divine Feminine that came through her, Jo Jayson has created a guidepost of love—a love that begins within. With each stroke of her paintbrush, each amazing Goddess revealed more of herself and brought forth her individual messages of healing and love. The stunning images that emerged contain a beauty and resonance that is felt in the heart.

Self-Love through the Sacred Feminine is a book to be savored and cherished; it is a feast for the eyes and the soul. It is a pathway of healing through the wisdom teachings of the Divine Feminine that have come to awaken the Divine Feminine within us all.

—Gail Swanson
The Heart of Love: Mary Magdalene Speaks
www.theheartoflove.com

Introduction

Whenever we embark on a task that honors our own souls, we create a space that allows us to heal, grow, and evolve.

The creation, therefore, becomes that of a sacred task, because our *souls* are sacred. We tend to think of sacred things as being outside of ourselves, like churches, houses of worship, ancient sites, and special objects. But the truth is, there is nothing more sacred to us than our own souls. Our souls are so special, holy, and precious, yet we often ignore or forget to acknowledge them, or have no connection to them whatsoever. More often than not, we treat ourselves with such disrespect and disregard that we unknowingly commit daily sacrilege.

Before we embark on the wisdom of the Sacred Feminine, I will explain to the best of my ability what this energy is.

The Sacred Feminine is what some call the Divine Feminine, or the Goddess. The Goddess is the feminine aspect of the Divine, of humanity, of life, and of creation itself. As women, we are expressions and representations, extensions, and reflections of this feminine energy. Likewise, men are expressions of the masculine aspect of the Divine.

To touch briefly and very simply on these aspects of the Divine as a whole, we must first understand its nature. Knowing and understanding that there is One Consciousness, One Source, or One Creator/God, we can comprehend that this "Oneness" is whole and complete in itself. This "Source" is what I refer to throughout this book as "Spirit." In order to experience itself in a different way on the earthly plane, this One Consciousness divided into two, much like an amoeba. These two aspects of the whole became what we understand as the masculine and feminine aspects. We use these words to describe the varying attributes that make up these two parts of the whole.

In nature, we see the masculine and feminine aspects of vegetable and plant life. Like animals, as humans we have gender-specific bodies but are in fact made up of both masculine and feminine aspects. Simply put, our bodies are expressions of one aspect, either masculine or feminine, but our souls consist of both, because our souls are extensions and expressions of the whole—the Oneness.

The masculine and feminine aspects show themselves within us in many different ways. They are the active, striving, and motivated part of ourselves and that which is the more responsible, protective part of our nature. The masculine is also the thinker, strategist, intellect—the doer, provider and giver.

As its complement, the feminine is the passive, still, and receptive side of ourselves. It is the carer, compassionate and empathetic. It is the intuitive wisdom, as opposed to the intellect, the receiver as opposed to the giver, "being" rather than "doing," stillness as opposed to action.

Both men and women need a balance of both of these aspects to make up a full, functioning personality and character. At various times throughout the day and our lives, we need to focus on more of one aspect than the other, but we must always strive for balance.

Many speak of the "Return of the Divine Feminine," a time we are in right now. This describes the return of balance and harmony to a world and culture that is currently severely unbalanced due to the overbearing weight of a deeply distorted masculine.

We see greed, disruption, war, hate, and degradation because we have been living in a world where the feminine has been subjugated, denounced, and neither honored nor respected for centuries. Without its true counterpart next to it in perfect balance and harmony, what we see is a distorted, twisted, and unbalanced masculine. And an unbalanced masculine aspect is unable to show itself as the Divine Masculine without the feminine counterpart to balance it out.

This is why many are returning to the sacredness of the "Goddess" concept. Those who are called to help balance the scales are driving the return of the Divine Feminine, which is and will be the healing of our world that human consciousness has called in. This isn't about Goddess worship, but about understanding, embracing, and embodying the aspects of the Divine Feminine (love, compassion, forgiveness) so that the healing of this planet may begin.

My paintings in this book are expressions of the Divine Feminine. They represent—from varying times in history—ancient Goddess archetypes, courageous prophetesses, and women of incredible strength of heart.

With the dominance of patriarchal religions, we, as women, long for a maternal presence in our spiritual world. We hear the call of our ancient forgotten yet familiar Mother, and realize that we are living in a world that has degraded and disempowered us. In very ancient times the feminine was revered as a wise, loving, maternal, and compassionate energy. The two aspects of the Divine were honored respectively and seen in the God/Goddess worship of times gone by.

We now live in a society that doesn't put as much focus on teaching us the benefits of compassion, love, and forgiveness; instead, our world pushes us to compete, strive, and succeed.

This book is about reclaiming the lessons and wisdom of the Sacred Feminine and applying them to ourselves so that we can find peace, love, and contentment within, instead of looking outside of ourselves for the things we *think* we lack.

We are taught to seek love and approval from others, instead of within. Whether it be a prospective partner, a boss, or our parents, we are taught to make ourselves as beautiful as possible so that someone will be attracted to us. We are encouraged to be a certain way to get the approval of another and to receive their love in return for our beauty, suitability, or sense of duty.

When that love fades or is taken away, or their approval turns to disapproval, we feel heartbroken, empty, rejected, and often abandoned, unworthy, and unlovable.

Looking at this from a higher perspective, we see the folly in putting all the criteria for being worthy of love and approval on to another.

In truth, the sole responsibility for our sense of worthiness lies within the self. To master the art of filling one's own well is one's greatest lesson and accomplishment. Of course, we are products of our upbringings, and if we were not shown unconditional love and approval when we were young, it is more than likely we will suffer as adults with feelings of worthlessness and low self-esteem. But regardless of our beginnings, whether we think it fair or not, it still becomes our responsibility to be our own source of love, worth, and respect.

All relationships, whether parent, lover, friend, child, or colleague, are our biggest teachers, because they teach us about ourselves. Nothing else in our human experience has the power and wisdom to show us who we truly are. Every human being experiences this dynamic of relationship. It is because of this universal human experience that we can witness the other person as another soul just like ours. Every soul is learning lessons much like our own and shares emotions much like ours. In this realization, we understand that we are all mirrors of and for each other; we show each other our own truths.

If any of you have prayed, or belong to and follow a religion or spiritual practice, you will have had the experience of reaching out from your heart to an energy or being that you perceive to be higher, bigger, better, and more powerful than yourself. In that moment, you will have felt a belief that outside of yourself there is some kind of nucleus or center of powerful love that will come to your aid, forgive and love you unconditionally, and be your savior.

For the most part, we are correct; but in other ways, we are delusional. What we are correct about is that there *IS* a source made of unconditional love, forgiveness, and aid, which we can call upon at any time to help us on this human journey. What we are delusional about is that this source is only *outside* of ourselves.

If we take a cup of water from the ocean, bring it home, put it on our kitchen table, and take a good look at it, we can ask ourselves if that cup of water is any different from the ocean it came from. Has it changed in composition? Have the percentages and ratios of minerals, sodium, and natural elements in the water changed since you brought it to your house, or is it exactly the same as the ocean it came from? Without doubt, it *is* exactly the same; it is just now housed in a different body: the cup.

The same applies to you. *Your soul is a cup full of Source.* Your soul is made up of exactly the same stuff as its original Source, whether you call it God, the Creator, or the Divine. The only difference is that on this dense earthly plane, it is housed in your physical body. That precious Divine soul of yours— that *cup full of Source*—rests, abides, and can be found in your heart chakra, right in the middle of your chest. Your emotional heart is your center, your resting place—your direct connection to who you are, your precious and sacred soul.

It is my deepest, heart-felt intention that the images in this book paired with the channeled wisdom and teachings given to me along the way will bring profound healing, inspiration, and empowerment to those who wish to return to their natural state of loving the self. Humans struggle to love themselves; it's a universal affliction. Self-love is our birthright, and the journey back to it is a necessary endeavor to achieving peace, harmony, and abundance of all kinds in our lives.

May the journey back to your self be a wildly wonderful, compassionate adventure.

Heartburst, 2010.

1

THE QUEEN

Self-Love, Self-Honor, and Self-Respect

Legends and mystery surround Guinevere like no other, painting her in many roles—brave Welsh Queen; beautiful, soulful lover; adulteress; victim; warrior; scholar; May Queen; and ethereal Goddess.

Guinevere was the Queen of King Arthur. Her Power and influence were so strong that it was widely believed that without Guinevere by his side, Arthur's legitimacy as King was weakened.

In the stories and legends written 600 years after her time, she became known for her beauty and imagined love affair with Lancelot, but she was also noted for her innate regality and majesty. She was beloved, honored, and respected as a Queen and was the complement to the very masculine energy of King Arthur. Born of noble blood, she made it possible for Arthur to be the king and leader that he was.

The conflicting stories of Guinevere are often untrue and sensationalized. Literature and fiction love a fallen woman, and much was made about her supposed infidelity to King Arthur. However, the essence of Guinevere is that of majestic feminine and regal energy.

Guinevere's Celtic beauty and embodiment of the mystery of Avalon, together with her passion for her land and loves, are indeed what makes the legend of this Queen so enduring.

She is sometimes referred to as the "Flower maid, the Faerie Goddess of love and fertility," and is believed to be closely connected with the Faerie Kingdom and honored on the high holiday of Beltaine (May Day). Her name also means the "White One" or the "White Faerie" (or "ghost"). She brings together the energy and powers of the "otherworld" to the world of men and is considered complete in herself—a Triple Goddess, the ultimate Queen.

GUINEVERE'S
PRAYER AND MESSAGE

Light a candle, and as you breathe in and out, focus on my flame and remember who you are. A child and spark of the Divine, no more or less. Understand you are from majestic heights; you are born of royal love, in the truest form of regal magnificence. Feel yourself as this and believe it, for it is Truth. Remember to always hold yourself in high regard and honor, not in arrogance, but in strong yet humble memory of the Spirit, which you are made of and what you truly deserve. Respecting and honoring yourself shows others how to treat you. When we honor ourselves and embody our own majesty, we create the most glorious King/Queen-dom in which to live in.

Guinevere teaches us that we are our own Queens and sovereigns. As she states in her message, when we realize who we are and what we are born from, we can never again forget that we come from "majestic heights" and "regal stock." Being extensions and expressions of the Divine: how much more regal does it get?

We have Kings and Queens in our cultures because centuries ago it was believed that to be crowned and anointed (Heb. *Mashiach*—Messiah) meant you were the closest to God. We anointed, crowned, and honored other humans, believing that they were superior, of higher stock, and more Divine than ourselves. Sitting on a throne was symbolic of being in the gods' lap. Today in the Western world of the twenty-first century, we still have royalty only because of tradition, and the idea that another human is more Divine or significant because they wear a crown seems naïve and ludicrous to us. In remembering that we all come from this Divine majestic height, we must, therefore, also recall that we are our own *cups full of Source.*

Given that there is no sovereign higher than Source/the Creator/God, we can conclude that in our expressions of ourselves, we are *all* majestic and magnificent; it is our birthright.

Guinevere says that if you fail to understand this—if you fall short of honoring your own majesty—you dishonor yourself and show others how to dishonor you, as well. If you do not respect the magnificence of your own source, you disrespect yourself and demonstrate to others how to do the same.

Every woman is born with a crown on her head, because every woman is an expression of the Goddess—the Divine Feminine. Likewise, every man is born with a crown on his head because he is an expression of the Divine Masculine. It's not easy for a woman to learn to walk as if she is wearing a crown. Many of us bow our heads with shame and feelings of worthlessness, and when we do, clearly our crown will fall off.

However, with your head held high, not in arrogance nor superiority, but in the quiet knowing that you are someone special, you will begin to resonate with the idea that you are more than enough. *You are worth it!*

Throughout this book and its lessons, you will read a great deal about needing to take responsibility. This lesson is your first responsibility to yourself: to remember to wear that crown every single day and keep it from falling off. Guinevere tells us that we teach each other how to treat us by the way we treat ourselves. Therefore, if you wish to be honored and respected by others, *you* must bestow this honor and respect on *yourself.*

When we experience disrespect from another, we tend to blame others for our hurt. We feel slighted for not receiving the respect we desire.

Why are we given situations like this, where another person disrespects us and makes us feel so unworthy?

Our own souls choose a myriad of experiences and relationships in our lives with others to learn more about ourselves. Before we incarnate, we decide the structure of our lives. We lay out the stage and its players and the circumstances that will shape who we are to become. It is difficult for many to understand the concept of choosing one's own parents and circumstances, particularly if those parents and circumstances were less than pleasant. For many, the idea that we may have chosen our own suffering is uncomfortable.

However, the soul's purpose for incarnating into the physical is to grow, expand, and become more of itself. In the hurt and rejection, the betrayal and abandonment, the childhood abuse and lack of love, there is created a framework. A situation is created from years of the same experience, but at some point— usually in one's adult life—we are faced with and given a golden opportunity of healing and growth.

The experience of hurt and disrespect gives us the clue to what is missing in our own vibration. In other words, we are given an imaginary mirror, and there we see the truth of our own belief system. Usually there is one last experience where our hearts and souls cry out, "No more!" or "Enough is enough!"

In essence, if we are being mistreated by another, we are being asked to look at ourselves and see how we have co-created this scenario with the other. When we look closely, we can see it is in the absence of respecting and honoring our own selves that we have set up the experience of another mirroring our own vibration. It is worthy to note that this setup was years in the making.

This concept may anger some, because they may not want to take responsibility for their own experiences; they may want to continue to blame the other. And yet this act keeps us securely locked in victimhood, leaving us in danger of missing the very precious clue being shown to us.

Once again, the "clue" is found in the way we dishonor and disrespect ourselves. Some may ask, "How could we have dishonored and disrespected ourselves if another is doing the disrespecting? What is it we are doing (or not doing) to create a situation where another is dishonoring us?"

We are all products of our upbringing; none of us can escape that. Some have more positive childhoods than others, depending on what each soul is required to learn in each lifetime. Everyone has a setup, and it usually isn't until deep into adulthood that we have the strength or awareness to look back and uncover where we absorbed and took on damaging belief systems, which then created unwanted experiences in our lives as adults.

The clue that the unwanted experience provides usually shows us that we have forgotten who we are—we have forgotten that we are our own *cup full of Source* and our own majesty. This appears in the way we talk to ourselves—our "mind talk." How often do we berate ourselves for failing or missing the mark? How often do we judge ourselves for not being good enough, clever enough, or beautiful enough? Staying humble is important, but demeaning ourselves leads to disrespect of the self.

We disrespect ourselves when we refuse to allow ourselves to follow our heart's path, when we do what others wish for us and disregard our own wishes, when we give ourselves to another who is not worthy of us, and when we feel smaller or less than others.

We dishonor ourselves when we lie to ourselves about a situation, a relationship that is glaringly not right for us, a job that does not fulfill us, or a friendship that is a one-way street.

We dishonor and disrespect ourselves when we feed ourselves junk food; when we are ashamed of our bodies, hiding them; when we can't look at our bodies in the mirror. Why is this such a dishonor? Because the body is our holy vessel that holds our sacred soul.

We disrespect the self when we don't stand up for ourselves, allowing others to make us feel unworthy, and when we surround ourselves with people who bring us down or refuse to celebrate us. We dishonor ourselves when we stay in unhealthy situations and are too scared to change.

Once we make the shift to remembering who we really are and embodying that majesty and honor for ourselves, our energies and beliefs begin to shift and transform. When we achieve the true understanding of who we really are, our energy brightens and rises, and our aura transcends to a higher, elevated vibration. Once this happens and we have finally shifted, we begin to demonstrate to others how to treat us. In honoring our own selves, we teach others how to honor us; we reset the stage and the experience to the way we want it to be, because we are now giving off the correct vibrations.

In each lifetime we are given these opportunities to evolve upwards to the next, higher level. We have the choice to remain stuck in our experiences; we have the choice and free will to remain victims to our life structure. Likewise, we have the choice and free will to rise above our circumstances and break the chain of hurt, abuse, unworthiness, and disrespect. How many generations of families have continued to teach the next generation the same misguided, painful beliefs? In each moment, we are given that opportunity to break the chain for our own children.

FOR GUINEVERE'S LESSON

These exercises can be done with a notebook and pen
when you have time to reflect.

- Can you remember a time in your life when someone disrespected and dishonored you? If it is more than one person, please list them as you remember them. List briefly next to each name how they disrespected you.

- Now list next to these experiences how it made you feel. What was the emotion that you felt during or after?

- Now list next to that if you still feel these emotions are true.

- Write a letter (you do not need to send it) to all those who have disrespected you, speaking your truth and acknowledging the actions committed against you. Include the feelings and beliefs you took on as a result. You may burn this letter at any point after to release the negative emotions.

- Remember a time when you disrespected and dishonored yourself. Examples: in a relationship, a job, ignoring your own heart and wishes, with your body, sexually, etc. If you can, recall how you felt about yourself during those times.

- Next, write a letter to yourself at any age and apologize to that version of yourself for not giving the respect and honor you deserved. Then explain why you did this, and forgive yourself for not knowing what you know now.

- List as many times as you can when you did remember to honor and respect yourself. Examples: Standing up for yourself, protecting your body from being used and abused, leaving an unhealthy or unhappy situation/ relationship that no longer served you, etc.

- Can you remember how you felt when you honored and respected yourself? Did those feelings last, or did you fall back into old, damaging beliefs?

- Remember a time when you dishonored and disrespected another person, such as a spouse or partner, a friend, boss or colleague, a stranger, etc. How did that make you feel, and why do you think you did it? Were you feeling less of yourself than you should have?

- In the days following these exercises, honor and pay respect to three people in your life. This could be as simple as buying them flowers, or saying how much they mean to you, or showing them their own sacredness in some way.

- Then do three things for yourself to acknowledge how much you honor and respect the woman that you are. These three things might include buying yourself a special gift, feeding yourself healthy food, or standing up for yourself in a challenging situation.

- Imagine every day that you are wearing your crown; remember that each time you lower your head in shame or blame or fear, your crown will fall off. Go easy on yourself and be gentle, but be very mindful of your "self-talk."

2

Mariamne of Magdala

THE MAGDALENE

Embracing the Sacred Feminine within Yourself

A BRIEF HISTORY OF THE MAGDALENE

Mariamne of Magdala—the Magdalene. Mysterious, misunderstood, and misrepresented, Mariamne (Greek: *Mary*) has been portrayed as a tempting prostitute, repentant sinner, trusted confidante, apostle, saint, and Goddess. Her story is so intriguing and shrouded with veils of mystery and sacred symbolism, it comes as no surprise that the woman and her life have been researched, depicted, and debated for so long.

Through analyzing the ambiguity of the Holy Grail, the Rose, the Holy Bloodline, and other references, it is widely thought and believed that this independent Jewish girl from the small fishing village of Magdala was indeed the "Beloved" of Yeshua (Jesus). It is believed that in witnessing his "Resurrection" she became the "Apostle to the Apostles," and the "one" to take the then-controversial and fragile teachings of Jesus outwards into the world, building the foundations of ancient Christianity.

Popular belief is that she carried Jesus' child (and thus the Holy Bloodline) in her womb as she fled to France; this child then became the ancestress to the French Merovingian Kings. Gnostic belief is that just as Yeshua/Jesus was the human embodiment of the Male Divine Messiah, Mariamne was the embodiment of the Sacred Feminine—the Goddess Messiah, consort and Bride of the Christ, and equal female counterpart to the Male Godhead.

Mariamne was canonized by the Catholic Church as a saint in 1969, in spite of the fact that Pope Gregory the Great had denounced her as a sinner and prostitute in 591. But whatever one believes or understands Mariamne of Magdala to be, this woman was surely a sacred sister of wisdom, a prophetess, and a High Priestess, who many believe taught Jesus the secret wisdom of the ancients. Brave leader, loyal disciple, and the perfect receptacle to spread the Divine "Word," her wisdom, goodness, and forgiveness, and her fearless story of loyalty and vision in a world where women had no worth, provides us in modern times with a role model of empowerment, healing, and strength.

THE MAGDALENE'S
PRAYER AND MESSAGE

With your breath, now, dear one, allow yourself to inhale all my love and light and exhale any darkness. We know that darkness cannot survive in the light, so allow yourself to absorb my love and light into your being, so that all manners of sorrow, hurt, or sadness dissipate in the glory of my brightness. I am one of the many faces of the Divine Feminine and I awaken your own ability to love yourself and others, to feel compassion, and to tap into your own intuitive wisdom. Have compassion for your own fragility, but be aware of the glorious strength that lies in the depths of your own heart. This strength—this awareness in your heart space—is called Love. It is what you are born of and from, and what you are learning to give to yourself. Fill your heart space with all my light that I pour into you now, and feel that overflowing and infinite supply of love shining out from the center of your chest. Remember, love is light; light is love, an endlessly flowing river of gifts and blessings.

As women, we are blessed to have beautiful, soft, sensuous bodies, which are so much of what we attribute to the "feminine." We are blessed to have breasts to nurture a child and give pleasure to ourselves and others. We have the ability to create a life inside us, the capacity to hold so much compassion and love for our children and those in our care. As women, we embody the *Sophia* (Greek: wisdom, the intuitive, and innate feminine wisdom). It's a privilege to be a woman.

The Magdalene has led the march of the Divine Feminine for many years. Her following amongst women finding empowerment and healing is remarkable, and the mystery surrounding her story as it slowly comes to light is compelling to women not only within the walls of religion, but also outside of these boundaries. As a beautiful and strong woman of immense faith and devotion, she is a representation of the glories of womanhood.

It is understood now in most secular circles that the Magdalene was Yeshua's beloved wife and partner. It is also understood that she held as much wisdom, sacred knowledge, and teachings as Yeshua/Jesus himself. Spiritualists agree that the "Christ Consciousness" or "God Consciousness" was held by both.

The Magdalene's message is twofold: first, it is time we as women celebrate the fact that we *are* women. In this life, our soul decided to show itself through the feminine. How glorious, beautiful, and powerful it is to be an expression of the Goddess. After centuries of being made to feel ashamed to be female, we are now being asked to rise and shine brighter in the truth of our womanhood.

In this manifestation of woman, we represent creativity, love, compassion, intuition, and incomparable wisdom. In our bodies we contain the greatest capacity to love. Not only are we receivers and vessels of love, we house and carry the body of another's soul in our womb; because of this, our innate nature is to love. The Magdalene teaches us not only to embrace our womanhood, beauty, sensuousness, and femininity, but also to live within that natural well of love in the heart.

We have already discussed that your soul resides in your heart space. The soul is pure, unconditional love. Thus, when we say "live in (or from) your heart," this means live, act, speak, and give from a place of unconditional love. Living from the heart also means receiving from a place of unconditional love; your intentions, choices, and decisions must all come from that same place. Unconditional love means exactly that: love with no conditions.

Living like this is not an easy task. Everything we have been taught by our parents, teachers, society, and culture lacks the element of unconditional love. It is an uncomfortable new dynamic to find ourselves in. And yet, each and every one of us *desperately* yearns for it.

We yearn for it because it is our true nature and what we are born from. We long for that feeling of home, of being held and loved unconditionally, no questions asked.

To live from the heart is a mindful exercise because our minds are liars. Our training as humans has taught us to listen to our minds instead of our hearts, and that's where we trip up every time. To be able to live from the heart, we must be mindful of our hearts; they are giving us constant clues via emotions, which act as our truths. It's the most wonderful GPS guidance system that we can possibly have.

Living from the heart means accessing your *cup full of Source* and being in that space. In practicing this, you will lessen and quiet the ego ramblings of the mind. Living from the heart means remembering how sacred you are and realizing and understanding all beings are sacred. It means that you understand the holiness of your source and essence, and you see and understand it in everyone—and everything—else.

Once we realize that our hearts house our *cup full of Source,* we begin to understand that we have our own source of unconditional love. Our soul is complete, never empty and never lacking; it is pure and infinitely overflowing with unconditional love. When we nurture and love our own being, the heart opens up like a rosebud in bloom. Much like the recycling symbol, as it overflows with our own love, we automatically send out love vibrations to those outside of ourselves. By sending out these love vibrations from our own full heart, others feel and receive it and wish to give it back in kind. The universe hears and feels your love vibration and sends it back to you. This is the law of the universe.

When you shut down your heart due to sadness, rejection, or fear, and when you protect your heart too much, you close off the flow of love from yourself and others to your heart. This creates an energetic barrier across the heart, with neither love coming in nor love going out; it's one of the many reasons people have heart attacks.

But when we allow the heart to be filled with our own self-love, we can easily give others unconditional love. When we are running on empty and have not filled our own well, we have nothing of value to give. In fact, we end up giving either nothing at all or love with conditions.

Conditional love is filled with expectations. We give to receive, because in some way we still feel empty, and we hope that in giving to another we can be filled up and our needs can be met.

We have all played out the dynamic of "I will love you *if* you love me"; "please love me, I need you, I can't live without you"; "my heart is broken because you did not love me"; or "I am unlovable if you don't love me." Whether we feel this way or another creates this dynamic with us, all of us have witnessed this conditional love in our lives.

Given this information, we may begin to look at our lives and ask ourselves "When and who have we loved unconditionally, and who have we loved with conditions? Have we ever received unconditional love, or only conditioned love?"

If you have a pet, you will have been loved unconditionally. Our pets are the main source of endless, effortless unconditional love. Some believe that we naturally love our children unconditionally, but this is not true. If you have been a child of parents who loved you with conditions and expectations, you will have been programmed to love your own children this same way. It is only with acute awareness that one can break the cycle of conditioned love; if you can do this, you will give the greatest gift to your children.

It is a great exercise to ask yourself how being loved unconditionally and conditionally has shaped your belief system and relationships. Unconditional love has the power to wrap someone in a blanket of acceptance, allowance, and forgiveness, to heal all wounds and soothe our broken hearts. This kind of love, when given to the self, has the power to move mountains in one's own healing. Unconditional love of the self is fundamental to the self-love practice.

As women, we are powerful. Not only is our beauty and feminine attributes potently compelling, but we have the Divine gift of loving. This is the most powerful gift of all. To love another because we recognize their divinity is a gift that can set everyone free. To love yourself because you recognize your own divinity will be your salvation.

Reflections
FOR THE MAGDALENE'S LESSON

These exercises can be done with a notebook and pen
when you have time to reflect.

- Buy yourself pink roses. Find ones that have a beautiful fragrance. Focus on them and allow yourself to understand your connection with them as an Expression of the Goddess. The pink roses will represent your beauty, power, allure, and love of being a woman.

- Try to remember a time when you were shown or given conditional love. It may be more than once; it may be each of your relationships. List them out and write a few memories of how this conditional love was shown to you.

- Next to this list, write how this made you feel. What was the belief and false truth that you took on from having been given conditional love? List all the false beliefs.

- When you look at these false beliefs, can you see that those who gave them to you had those false beliefs in themselves?

- Acknowledge, accept, and allow these memories and experiences to be. See the truth in them without becoming angry or resentful; just allow them to be.

- Looking at this list, ask yourself if you still hold these beliefs and write down next to it if you really feel that they are true.

- Now remember a time when you were shown unconditional love in any of your relationships, which can also include pets or strangers. List them out if you can.

- How did that gift of unconditional love make you feel? List these feelings out.

- Next to this list of feelings, ask yourself if you still feel the same and if you believe it is true

- In the days following this exercise, focus on your *cup full of Source.* Be mindful of giving and receiving, doing and being from a place of unconditional love. Notice how it will soften you, and how all resistance to that which does not please you falls away and there is a gentle allowing of people, places, and things just being as themselves.

3

Brighid

MOTHER GODDESS OF IRELAND

Flowing with the Cycles and Changes of Life and Womanhood

A BRIEF HISTORY OF
BRIGHID

Brighid (Naomh Bríd, Bride, Brigida, Brigit; also called "Mary of the Gael") is the Triple, Mother Goddess of Ireland, but her following and influence is also found in Scotland (Bride), England (Brigantia), and in other forms around the British Isles and western Europe. The Romans called her Minerva, and the Greeks knew her as Athena. She maintained many realms and was known as the Goddess of fertility and midwifery; she was also said to "birth in" Spring, representing new life.

Brighid is a Goddess of the Sun and Fire, much like the Roman Vesta, bringing warmth and safety to home and hearth. She purifies and heals through the element of fire, like Pele. She also rules the moon, the magical realms of inspiration and poetry, and various crafts, including smithwork and weaving. Her close connection to the cycles and energy of nature makes her the perfect Goddess of healing and plant medicine.

The Triple Essence of this Goddess denotes the Maid, Mother, and Wise One (Crone)—all aspects of womanhood. When Christianity moved its way into pagan Ireland and the Celtic regions, loyalty to Brighid was so strong and intertwined in daily life and culture that the Church incorporated her with the Abbess Brigid of Kildare, who they later canonized as a Saint to satisfy the people.

Throughout the centuries, the stories of both Saint and Goddess have become so inextricably interwoven that it is nearly impossible to disconnect them, and even in present day they are bound.

In ancient times, the Daughters of the Flame—nineteen virgin priestesses—tended to Brighid's Eternal Flame at the Fire Temple in Cil Dara (Kildare). Today, a group of devoted nuns known as the Brigidine Sisters continue to tend the fire—called *Solas Bhride* (the Light of Brighid).

In Ireland and throughout many parts of the world, Imbolc (meaning "in the belly") or St. Brigid's Day (Candlemas) is celebrated on February 1st and 2nd as a welcoming of new life and the homecoming of the Sun after the long winter days.

Brighid is considered the female counterpart of Lugh the Ildana; she is also, with her protective, warrior energy, a counterpart of Archangel Michael. Regardless of whether one honors her as Goddess, Saint, or both, Brighid can be called upon to ignite the eternal spark of new life, inspiration, healing, and protection.

BRIGHID'S
PRAYER AND MESSAGE

Breathe deep, in and out, and open your heart to the warmth that I offer you. As my flame burns eternally, know that you are kept warm by my love for you and that your cares and worries are burnt away by the brightness of my Light. Your own heart carries this flame; it is the eternal Light of your soul. Just as nature has its own cycle of seasons, so do we move through our own natural cycles of life. We each have our own summer time to shine; our own autumn to let go and release; our own winter to rest and be quiet; and our own spring to rebirth and renew. Relax and allow yourself now to flow in the natural cycle of your own spiral of being. You are protected and supported, and in this comfort, connect to your own spark and flame to create healing, inspiration, and oneness with nature.

Brighid's energy is like a spiral, ever-flowing in essence, like the seasons. If we observe the four seasons, we notice that plants and animals will hibernate in winter, emerge and give birth in spring, flourish in summer, and harvest in autumn. Nature is perfectly aligned with the rhythm of her energy and the creative force of the universe, and we are encouraged to embody its cycles—emulating the way nature flows, unresisting with the seasonal energies and their changes—so that we might align ourselves with its wisdom.

Brighid talks about being one with nature. Many of us do this without conscious thought; we stay warm resting inside during winter in a kind of quiet reflection, and then we emerge in the spring feeling renewed, hopeful, and ready to take on new projects. In the summer we become more active, carefree, and invigorated, spending much more time outside in the sunlight. During autumn we naturally start to gather ourselves up, getting ready for the holidays and settling down for the winter months again. Our rhythms are automatic, so following the patterns of the seasons gives us a feeling of security and stability.

However, as Brighid says, we also have our own personal seasons. These include times when we have shone brightly, been active and productive, and been seen in our best light. We call this our personal summer. Times when we wanted to start a new job, diet, look, or lifestyle—this is our personal spring. Chapters in our lives when we let people and places go, needing to shed skin and witness an ending under specific circumstances—this is our personal autumn. Then there are times when we have felt unwell, tired, or just needed to quietly rest from the outside world—this is our personal winter.

As women, we also experience the cycles of the varying stages of womanhood. Brighid's identity as the "Triple Goddess" is multi-layered and carries several different meanings. But in essence, it allows us to see and witness Brighid in the three stages of womanhood: Maiden, Mother, and Crone.

Throughout our lives, we will experience challenges as we pass through the varying stages of womanhood. Our youth (Maiden) can be a tumultuous time, full of mistakes and hard-learned lessons; yet it also denotes the peak of our physical beauty, freedom, and hope for the future.

The mother stage obviously expresses a time to nurture our children. Even if we do not have children, it marks a time when we become less self-engrossed, moving into a phase when we give of ourselves and care for another. This stage offers many blessings and gifts, but it also has its challenges. Loss of freedom, loss of the self, and intense periods of caring for another can cause resistance and depression in many. Our biggest growth comes during this point, when we are interacting, forging, and deepening our relationships.

Finally, there is the time of the Wise One (Crone), where we move away from focusing on others into a stage of wisdom gained from experience and look out with a renewed, seasoned intelligence of how we fit into our own personal lives and the world outside of ourselves. It is during this time that we feel a true sense of who we are and mellow into our own truths. For some women, this stage can be the most challenging, as we move into a loss of youth, our bodies change, and those in our care move on. We are asked to look at ourselves and re-evaluate all that we have lived up till now. Yet for many other women, the Crone stage is the most liberating; it allows them to focus on themselves again, but from a quieter, wiser perspective.

We often go into mourning at the loss of a cycle—the loss of a particular stage of our lives and womanhood. Mourning is good; it helps release that which no longer serves us, but becomes problematic if we do not let these stages go with a sense of gratitude and acceptance.

When I became a mother unexpectedly, I put up a lot of resistance to this new cycle that I suddenly found myself in. With every ounce of my being I resisted the changes in my body. I hated the way my body felt and looked during my pregnancy; I was afraid of motherhood and the idea of being responsible for a new, fragile life. I mourned the loss of my freedom and the plans I had for myself. Life was now in charge, and I wasn't consciously privy to the "plan." Nor was I mentally prepared for motherhood. In my resistance to it, I suffered deeply with depression; hormones and a very traumatic labor did nothing to help the way I felt. It was as though I was swimming upstream, struggling to keep my head above water.

Yet for many, pregnancy, birth, and motherhood is a time of gleeful celebration. Eventually, I arrived at those emotions, too, with much help and patience. I look back on those early years as a mother now with complete gratitude and a deep sense of love and joy. In fact, I wouldn't change a second of it, but I can see how my resistance to it served neither me nor my baby at the time.

Now as my children begin to leave the nest, I am entering a new stage of being—a new cycle of womanhood. This time, I am mindful of my resistance and understand that in the emergence of menopause and the next half century of my life, there will be aspects of myself that I need to let go of. At the same time, the opportunity for my accrued wisdom to create a new and blossoming version of myself is immense.

Learning to move fluidly through your life—without becoming fixed at one point—and learning to allow things to flow and change is being one with nature's cycles. In this "allowing" you will find greater peace than if you resist, and your body will react more gently.

In each of the cycles of womanhood—like the seasons—we can find inspiration, comfort, and jeweled blessings of wisdom.

When I painted Brighid, I was guided to include multiple spiral patterns in order to represent her energy. This also reflects our non-linear lives. Our lives move, grow, and expand in a spiral motion. Indeed, we all tend to have many experiences spiraling above a situation we have already experienced, repeating each time from a slightly higher perspective and with a newer wisdom.

The patterns of nature and sacred geometry share this spiral motion; if you have ever witnessed the miraculous unfolding of plant stems and leaves or the blooming of a flower, you will know what I mean. We each have our own spiral path that moves and flows above and around, giving us opportunities to learn, heal, release, and become more. We all know that when we don't learn our lesson, we go through it again and again until we finally get it.

Allow yourself to go with the flow of events and to not put up resistance to that which you are experiencing. Permit change to move and evolve you and embrace all stages of where you find yourself to be. This not only allows the universe and your soul to bequeath to you all that you need—whether it be a lesson, healing, a new opportunity, a relationship, or a new location—but it also allows you to be in alignment with your highest, most authentic self. This is an act of Self-Love. Remember that your soul is leading the way; your ego has free will to keep screwing up if it doesn't take notice, but the goodness and blessings that are vested and waiting for you to experience them are released in the flow of non-resistance.

FOR BRIGHID'S LESSON

These exercises can be done with a notebook and pen
when you have time to reflect.

- Can you remember having trouble emotionally or physically with a new stage or cycle of life? What resistance did you put up?

- How did resisting this new cycle make you feel, and how could you have made it easier for yourself?

- Recall a time when you DID embrace a new cycle of change; was it easier than if you had resisted it?

- What other areas of your life do you offer up resistance to? Can you list ways that this makes your experience more difficult?

- How can we align better with nature's cycles and seasons? What can we do, in the wisdom of winter, spring, summer, and autumn, that will reap all the blessings and jewels of these seasons? As we move into the next season, what can you plan for yourself that aligns with the energy of that season and what it has to teach us?

- What have you experienced that allows you to see the spiral motion of life? Try and remember situations or experiences where you have spiraled around again and again, each time with a slightly higher perspective. Do you feel you have learned the lesson this stage of your journey was trying to teach you?

- In the days ahead, be mindful when you are pushing against and resisting a situation you find yourself in. See it, feel it, and notice how it may be making that experience so much more difficult than it needs to be. Notice also that by holding this resistance you may be blocking your emotions, as well as that which the universe and your soul is wanting to bequeath you via this experience.

- Practice a day or a week of non-resistance and notice the consequences in your reality. Do this exercise for all the seasons coming up for you in the next twelve months.

ONE WHO IS ALL

*Internal Power, Empowerment, and Taking Your
Power Back*

A BRIEF HISTORY OF
ISIS

Isis (Greek form of the Egyptian *Ast* or *Aset*, meaning "Throne" or "Throne-Mother of the Gods") is known as the Goddess of All Goddesses. A story is told of Aset (Isis) coming down from the constellation of Sirius to rule and secure the present seed race in the Land of Khem (Chem), which is present-day Egypt. The word "alchemy" is thought to be derived from "Khem," tying Isis inextricably with the experience of magic and manifestation.

Isis embodies the empowered Divine Feminine. Her realm absorbed many of the principle Goddess attributes in Egypt, but she began as an independent deity in pre-dynastic times around the Nile Delta. There are many versions of the story of Isis and her husband, Osiris, who was also referred to as her "brother" (in ancient Egyptian and Semitic cultures, the terms "brother" and "sister" were not always literal; in fact, most times they were terms of endearment for both first cousins and spouses). Perhaps the best-known tale of Isis's life is that of the violent death of Osiris, and how she, in her grief, transformed into a hawk and hovered over his body, fanning her wings to bring breath and life back to his body.

Isis became known as the Mother of Life and the Crone of Death; interestingly, the image of her son, Horus, nursing from her breast was the original iconic image, which later inspired the painting of the *Madonna and Child*. Pharaohs used the metaphor of "sitting in the lap of Isis" in order to bequeath from her their own desired majesty and divinity. To "sit in the lap of Isis" was to inherit her throne.

Isis's loyalty and worship spread to Greece, Rome, and pagan cultures throughout Europe and the Middle East. Jesus and the Magdalene were believed to be schooled in the Mysteries of Isis, which Plato thought to be over 10,000 years old in his day.

Isis Panthea—the Lady of 10,000 Names. Goddess of Life, Death, Rebirth, the Moon, the Sun, Healing, and Magic, the absolute Mother and Woman Divine . . . this is Isis—*One Who Is All*.

ISIS'S
PRAYER AND MESSAGE

Breathe in and out deeply, and find that center where your power resides. Internal and authentic power lie in your solar plexus and are felt as truth in your heart. As you connect with this power within you, know and understand that you are responsible for what you create and manifest in your own world around you. Believe in your own power of creation so you can truly focus on manifesting only things you wish and desire—for the good of yourself and others. With my gentle, loving, yet powerful Light, I shine on you now to allow you to see the brilliance of your own magnificence and claim your own personal power and authority. Magic is the manifestation of focused intention; it is the witnessing of the miraculous. It is what you have at your own fingertips to create if you can focus, align, and understand that you are a co-creator with this magical universe.

Isis is as powerful as her reputation. She is the all-encompassing, all-powerful, and all-supreme Egyptian Goddess of rebirth, magic, and fertility. The entire image I created of her was painted onto of a layer of gold leaf because her energy is that of a profound, golden vibration. Her elegance and poise caught my attention when I felt her, and that is what I tried to express on the canvas. She possesses immense internal power—an unshakable confidence within that gives off a serene, yet invincible essence. Unlike external power, which is about the gain of material and outside accomplishments, internal power is much stronger and less likely to be taken away once it is established.

Isis comes to teach you about your own power. In my chakra workshops and teachings we discuss that personal, internal power resides in your solar plexus. The element is fire, and the color is the golden yellow of the sun. When working with Isis's energy, one needs to focus directly *within* the solar plexus.

The first step, therefore, to understanding how to use your own personal power is to know *where* to find it. The solar plexus can be found below your sternum and above your belly button. In this lesson, you will come to understand not only how to locate and use this personal power, but also how to avoid losing it or giving it away.

Far too many women throughout history, and even now in the twenty-first century, have been conditioned by society and culture to give their power away. Sadly, many of us do not even realize we *have* our own internal power; it is not something we are taught by parents or teachers. In fact, it is likely that neither our parents nor teachers are even aware of it themselves.

Internal power is not given the same frenzied focus as acquiring more money, property, land, and higher positions. It is usually as an adult, after many experiences of feeling powerless, that one begins to focus within and realize one's own light is diminished.

No one can truly take your power from you. We sometimes say, "they took my power away," but this isn't true. Stealing someone's internal power is very difficult to accomplish, unless of course *you* leave the door to your power center wide open for anyone to come in and steal that which is rightfully yours.

We can allow and subconsciously invite anyone on the lookout for a weak, unassuming participant to help themselves to our power. We do this for two reasons: first, we may not be aware we have our own power, and second, in our innocence and unknowing, we allow ourselves to feel intimidated by another.

Self-confidence, self-esteem, and self-worth are the aspects and flavor of the solar plexus—the power chakra. Notice the emphasis on the word *self;* how we feel about ourselves and the way in which we emit this feeling into the world is what determines whether we are perceived to be a confident, successful person, or a weak, vulnerable victim.

It's helpful to think of our power center as a room in the temple of our body where we can choose to go and switch on all the lights. In visualizing this, we can decide whether we want the lights on at full strength or gently dimmed. Likewise, we can also decide if we want to shut the door and store the key in a safe place or leave it open, unlocked, and vulnerable.

Knowing and understanding that our internal power center is *our* responsibility, at *our* command, is key to using our power wisely. Consciously keeping the fire stoked each day is imperative to making sure our body is lit with the brilliant energy of self-confidence.

Throughout this book, I discuss self-responsibility. This is because it's a vital component in healing and empowering oneself, and a powerful truth that is often forgotten. In order to never feel victimized again by another or their actions, *we* must be the ones who take responsibility to ensure this doesn't happen. Waiting for another to make you feel the emotion you long for is like waiting for Santa Claus to come down the chimney.

Understanding that our actions, beliefs, thoughts, and consequent realities are under *our* control and no one else's is fundamental to healing. Certainly, some things are already destined, but we have an *enormous* amount of free will, which puts the steering wheel in our hands. In other words, *you* possess the ability to direct your own life path; free will is your ticket to use for growth, or for stagnancy.

How brightly we shine, or how much light we "switch" on, directly affects how others see and perceive us. How we shine through our experiences—whether we choose to be charged up or running on low—will directly affect the happenings and manifestations of that day.

Our internal power *never* runs out—unless we choose not to recharge or take care of it. Your power comes from an infinite supply of Source. Let us not forget who we are: each of us is a *cup full of Source*. Source energy is not only infinite, but overflowing; it is all-powerful, the power of existence. Remembering this and reminding yourself that *you* are an extension and expression of this Source will ensure you never again forget that self-power is your birthright.

We can access this power by creative visualization:

Imagine that there is a ball of fire or light within your solar plexus. Intentionally see and feel this ball of light expand, shining its golden yellow light out of the very center of your body in all directions. See the light coming out of your solar plexus at the front, the sides, and the back of your body. Extend the rays of light as far out of the room and building as you can imagine. See yourself beaming now as a beacon of light; watch and notice how your posture changes with this fulfillment of internal power and light.

Focusing your intention to expand this light outside of yourself is the way to recharge. Make a concerted effort to do this every time you leave the house.

When you focus on the light in your solar plexus, it directs your energy to this center and activates it by your intention. Holding that visualization in your mind's eye allows you to stoke your own fire, power up, and shine as brightly as you can imagine.

Shining in your own light isn't about being loud and extroverted, however; it represents your self-confidence, knowing, and understanding the power that you have. When you are shining brightly like the star that you are, *no one* can diminish your light. It is only when *you* choose to let that light dim that you lose power.

Remember, personal power is *not* external. When we look outside of ourselves to attain power, applause, or approval, we set ourselves up for failure.

Consider a certain type of celebrity who goes into show business to achieve fame and attention. Becoming a "star" to be adored and applauded is his sole motivation; he looks outside of himself to achieve the approval and confidence he lacks so *desperately* on the inside. It is the only way he knows to achieve a sense of worth. When he comes offstage and the external spotlight is no longer shining on him, there is a terrible let down and deflation, because the outer source of his light has gone out.

When the outer source of light leaves us, we are faced with the reality of whether we have enough light within to feed our sense of self-esteem and value. When we lack the light within, we crash. This is why we see many young celebrities emotionally shattered and falling into depression or addiction. External power will *never* light your path.

When you are not fully charged up and shining, you cannot sense your own power. If you allow yourself to run on near empty, then you become a perfect target for those looking outside of themselves to take power and make themselves feel more *power-FULL*. This is what bullies do, because they themselves feel powerless and lack confidence; they steal other people's power via means of intimidation.

People who are truly and quietly confident have no need of intimidation tactics, and in fact will validate and hold up the vulnerable. A falsely confident person, on the other hand, is usually the one who will make an unconfident person feel like a speck on the floor. This is how intimidation works.

Looking at it this way, we can perceive that the bully and the victim have more in common than we may initially believe. Both are lacking in confidence and belief in their own internal power, but one has been taught to steal another's power to make themselves feel more powerful.

If we do not teach our children—particularly girls—that they have their own power center and are in control of their own confidence and worth, then our girls will continue to unknowingly give their power away to others. If we do not teach our boys that power is internal as opposed to external, we will find ourselves with yet another generation of males searching outside of themselves to gain the false, external power they feel they need. This historic and unending misconception is the ultimate catalyst for war.

Just as you power up and recharge your cell phone each day, remember to do this for *yourself*. Being full of light is the best way to move into your day; it will shift your dynamics with others and begin to infuse your manifestations with purpose and positive validation. This transforms you into an *empowered* creator.

Reflections
FOR ISIS'S LESSON

These exercises can be done with a notebook and pen
when you have time to reflect.

- Remember a time (or times) when you felt you had your power taken away from you. List them all out.

- Remember how you felt *before* that encounter or experience. Do you recall feeling vulnerable and weak, and lacking confidence? Notice that the other person who took your power—or more truthfully the one to whom you openly offered your power to—must have needed to take your power to make themselves feel more powerful. To the best of your ability, analyze the dynamic between both of you and see the truth in it.

- Remember times in your life when you *HAVE* stood in your own power, refusing to allow someone to intimidate you. List them out, and note how those occasions made you feel.

- Have *you* ever been the bully and intimidated another? If so, recall how you felt—were you feeling so low on internal power and confidence that you took the power of another to feel better about yourself? List these occasions, and ask yourself if it gave you what you were searching for.

- Perform the solar plexus creative visualization each day if possible, or as often as you can, to begin shifting your subconscious focus. Mornings are best before you start your day. Notice how you feel after the solar plexus visualization; take note of your posture. Do you feel a shift in how you hold yourself once you visualize yourself powered up?

- Stand facing the brightness of the sun: this will help charge up your own solar energy.

- Buy yourself sunflowers as a reminder to turn with your face towards the light.

5

Mary
THE MOTHER

Comfort and Support, Asking for Help, Self-Talk

Mary the Mother (Greek: *Mary*; Aramaic/Hebrew of the first century AD: *Maryam/Miriam*) was an ordinary Israelite Jewish girl from Nazareth in the Galilee. The little we know of her from sacred texts reveals that she was devout to the Jewish traditions of her family.

The Roman Catholic dogma of the Immaculate Conception is the belief that when Mary was conceived in the womb of her mother, Anne, she was cleared and free of all original sin, leaving her pure in sanctified grace.

This concept is not universally agreed upon throughout all corners of Christianity, but traditional Christian doctrine states that Mary was a virgin and that the miraculous, virginal conception of her son, Yeshua (Jesus), was proof that Yeshua was conceived via the planting of Divine seed into Mary's immaculate womb. It is also believed throughout much of Christianity that she remained a virgin thereafter.

Many Gnostics and scholars of mystical texts and those who have looked beyond the boundaries of Christianity, however, believe that Mary actually conceived *seven* children, including Yeshua. They believe she was betrothed and married to Joseph, and was for all intents and purposes the quintessential Jewish wife and mother.

The story of Yeshua and his suffering made it easy for others to empathize with his mother's subsequent suffering; thus, the Roman Catholic Church made her the symbol, face, and character of the Divine Mother. The doctrine of her Assumption and claim to the Throne of Heaven proclaimed her the Queen of Heaven, Queen of the Angels, and Divine Mother of God. The Eastern Orthodox Church calls her *Theotokos* (Greek: Mother of God) and holds similar doctrines to the Catholic Church.

What is interesting is that, over the centuries, she has taken on the roles of many pagan Mother Goddesses held before patriarchal religion was predominant in the world. Additional research reveals powerful connections with the *Shekinah* (Hebrew name for the feminine face of God) and the *Sophia* (Greek name for feminine Divine wisdom); both are deeply intertwined with Mary the Mother. She slowly took on the role as the Holy Spirit and the Divine Mother of All, realms and attributes also seen in Isis, Asherah, Inanna, and many other Mother Goddess archetypes from various cultures.

The dove, the lily, the concept of her wisdom, the throne on which she sits—all these originate from the idea of the Shekinah and can be seen in all preceding Mother Goddesses.

Many believe that Mary herself was a priestess of Isis/Asherah and taught Yeshua and Mary Magdalene the lessons of the Isis Mystery School. Many images of Isis and her son, Horus, suckling at her breast are widely thought of as the very first Madonna and child, which as we know became the most beloved representation of Mary and her son.

There is an interesting relationship between Mary and the angelic realm, not only because she is given the title Queen of Angels, but due to her close connection and association with Archangel Metatron (Enoch), who is considered the highest of angels and the Celestial Scribe.

Close association with the Chinese ancient Goddess of compassion and mercy, Guan Yin, is also very clear, and the symbolism of the lotus/lily and serpent/dragon make this association even stronger.

Whatever our beliefs about this incredible mother figure of compassion and love, and whichever part of the story we wish to hold on to, without doubt, this Lady Mary has become to so many *"a woman cloaked with the sun, with the moon under her feet and a crown of twelve stars above her head"* (Book of Revelation 12:1).

MARY'S
PRAYER AND MESSAGE

Breathe, my child. As you take the long inhale into your body, take in my love for you. As you exhale, release and let go of all that weighs you down. All of your worries and burdens can be given to me now, for I shall take them and transmute that heavy energy into Light. As you surrender yourself to me now, I will wrap you in my arms and cradle you while your mind and body take rest. Take this time now to feel my support and love for you, and know that all of your concerns are taken care of. There is no need to worry anymore, for all your prayers are heard and all are answered for the highest good, if you allow yourself to surrender them to me. Relax now, my dear child, into my arms, and allow yourself to be soothed.

MARY'S LESSON

Mother Mary was one of the most beautiful energies to channel and paint. She came to me as a middle-aged woman and immediately showed me her hand. Looking back on it now, I realize how brilliantly this represented the meaning of her message. If you look closely at my image of Mother Mary, you will see that her hand is out, open and palm up, almost asking to receive you. Simultaneously, the open hand is giving as well as receiving; this is the profound beauty and wisdom in Mary's message.

One of the beautiful aspects of being a woman is that we are innately maternal. Even if we do not, cannot, or choose not to have children, a woman's instinctive innate nature of caring is maternal in nature. When we think of maternal love, we think of being sheltered, held, soothed, comforted, nourished, and nurtured. Even if we did not receive this from our own mother, we know that this kind of love exists, and we have witnessed it.

There is a surrender and a release when we imagine being cradled by a maternal energy. We allow ourselves to let go of our burdens and allow another to soothe us. As women, we are adept in soothing, giving support, and caring for others. For many of us, it comes so naturally that we tend to do this for all those who need it. Yet in our efforts to come to the aid of those all around us, we rarely create time to give this care to ourselves.

Many women—mothers, especially—are running around caring for others and feeling depleted. Their batteries are running on low, and at the end of the day they often feel there is nothing left for them.

Women have gotten better over the decades in self-care. Time for bubble baths, massages, pedicures, girls' nights out, and of course, the odd yoga class—these things are more common now in my generation than they were in my mother's, but some women still have a problem reaching out for help when they need it. Striving for equality in society and the workplace, as well as juggling the roles of wife, mother, career climber, and supportive friend can create a mountain of problems in reaching out for support.

In my darkest hours I know *I* have struggled to call on a friend or ask for emotional support. Our weaknesses and vulnerable places within are uncomfortable to share for those who strive to be strong and independent.

It took many years for me to understand that great strength, courage, humility, and wisdom is only shown when we can lay bare our vulnerable broken bits to another. Surrendering into another's arms to be comforted when we are not able to comfort ourselves is a display of growth and emotional intelligence. Pride has no place on the path to healing.

If you are lucky enough to have a spouse, family members, close friends, or, dare I say, a mother who you can turn to for support and comfort, then I would strongly recommend you do so. Asking for help is an act of self-love; the reason for that lies in the balance and harmony created by the energy of giving and receiving.

As women and expressions of the Goddess, in our feminine essence we are deeply connected to the aspect of receiving. However, as I mentioned before, we tend to lean way too much into our masculine and spend our time giving too much of ourselves. Creating balance for *receiving* love by asking another to give to you is creating comforting, soothing, and much-needed harmony and alignment in your energetic system. Recognizing if there is an unbalance and deficit in your life of what you give out and what you receive is vital to creating harmony and peace within.

The other aspect of Mary's lesson is our self-talk and how it sounds when we are feeling less than perfect. For the majority of us, we can probably admit to ourselves and others that our self-talk is far from encouraging or nurturing. In fact, if we could record the inner mumblings of our minds on any given day, we would probably be shocked and somewhat disheartened at the lack of support we show ourselves.

For the most part, we beat ourselves up. We chastise ourselves when we miss the mark, and we really, really struggle with being kind to ourselves when we look in the mirror. All of us, at some time or another, have fallen victim to

being a victim. We can have the greatest of pity parties that last for days with piles of comfort food and other stimulants to help celebrate the pity. Pity parties can even be necessary if they last just one night, but for many, shutting down the pity party never happens, and we stay locked and stuck in a stagnant place of victimhood.

The energy of "why me, poor me, unlovable me" is familiar to many of us, but the truth is that this kind of vibration will keep us prisoner to a reality we don't want. The sooner we can pull ourselves out of this vibration the better.

Shifting to an energy that says "I deserve more than this because I am valuable" is the vibration that serves as a bridge to take us from the quagmire of "woe is me, I am wretched" to a vibration that says, "I can do this, I am able and worthy, I deserve it, and I am loved."

What we say to ourselves about our own sense of worth, accomplishments, failures, our bodies, and abilities has a direct connection to the realities we live in. Our relationships and dynamics with others show up in the same vein of vibration as does our self-talk. Watching how we talk to ourselves is vital for healing the self. Our cells, tissues, and organs hold the energy of our self-talk, beliefs, and thought patterns. Anything less than loving, supportive, and compassionate self-talk is setting ourselves up for disease and the breakdown of our health.

Most of us have taken on the belief systems of our parents and teachers. We inherit them, but we also absorb any damaging untruths hurled our way as children. These false truths become our absolute truths and can cause untold damage to our adult relationships and the way we parent our children.

If your self-talk does not resemble anything similar to healthy maternal love and support, it is time to change it. Affirmations, mantras, prayers, and healing the inner child are all ways to help shift ones inner conversation to a vibration that transforms your life for the better. Teaching our wounded subconscious to feel deserving, loved, supported, and grateful is the prerequisite to a *life* full of love, support, and gratitude.

Honoring the need for others in our lives to be there for us when we need them and honoring the self by changing our outdated and damaging self-talk record are the main ingredients for creating a soft place for ourselves to fall.

But there is also another area of support and comfort that eagerly awaits your call for help 24/7. Spirit/Source, angels, guides, God/Goddess—whichever resonates with you—are all waiting to offer help. It's not easy being Light Spirit energy in a dense physical body, but that's what we are, and the truth of the matter is that if you're reading this book, you have very likely already been awakened to that fact. It would serve us well to honor those in Spirit, and call home every so often. Asking Spirit's help to guide you through whatever you need, asking for comfort and respite, for clarity and intervention, are all requests that are eagerly waiting to be answered. Knowing that you are never alone and have an ongoing 24-hour support system set up in the non-physical is vital for anyone, especially those on the path to healing.

Calling out for help in prayer or meditation is your right and duty as a *cup full of Source*. It is amazing and quite magical to witness the way those in Spirit answer us after we have taken the time to connect with and include them in our lives. Source knows the truth of every situation and experience you are having, so it behooves you to call upon it for the support, comfort, and unconditional love you need.

Reflections
FOR MARY'S LESSON

These exercises can be done with a notebook and pen
when you have time to reflect.

- Consider and list the ways in which you give to others—family, friends, colleagues, neighbors. How does giving to them in the way that you do make you feel?

- Are there times when you feel resentful giving to others? If so, what is it that makes you feel resentful?

- Can you recall a time (or times) when you were in need of help, exhausted, or emotionally low and you did not reach out? List them if you can.

- Can you remember why you did not reach out? What was it? Shame? Pride? Feelings of worthlessness? Write down all the feelings you can remember that stopped you from asking another for help when you needed it most.

- Can you remember a time when you *DID* ask for help and reached out? What was the response? Did you get the help you needed? How did it make you feel?

- Name at least three people who helped you in the past. Where you able to receive their help and support freely and openly? And if not, why?

- In the days ahead, be extra mindful of how you talk to yourself. What do you say to yourself as soon as you wake up, as you are rushing around, accomplishing your tasks, dealing with challenges, and as you end the day before you go to sleep? Notice what kind of tone you are using with yourself. Be mindful of your thoughts, and if you need to shift any thought to a kinder one, do so immediately.

- Every morning, look at yourself in the mirror and say "Good morning, I love you, you are beautiful inside and out." Do this again in the evening whilst cleaning your teeth.

- Make a list for the week of all your achievements, however small. Keep it on your desk or phone or wherever might be convenient. On Sunday evenings at the end of each week, read them through and congratulate yourself. Get into the habit of praising instead of berating yourself.

- Read Mary's prayer every night before bed. Connect with her, and ask her to hold you in her arms as you sleep and to be by your side during the day. Even if you feel uncomfortable reaching out to Mary because you may have not done so before (or you are unfamiliar with her energy), attempt to do so anyway; the benefits of her energetic support will be greater than any of your doubts.

Jeanne d'Arc

MAID OF ORLÉANS

Finding Faith,
Courage, and Strength

A BRIEF HISTORY OF
JEANNE D'ARC

Jeanne d'Arc (Joan of Arc) is a beloved historical figure who people admire not only for her courage and faith, but also for her strength, in spite of her youth. She was a devoutly religious peasant child who was devoted to Jesus and Mary. At age thirteen, Jeanne began to hear voices and prophesies that she was to save her beloved France from the stranglehold of the English. The voices of Archangel Michael, St. Catherine of Alexandria, and St. Margaret of Antioch became so loud and frequent that in 1429, at the tender age of seventeen, she was moved to persuade the French army to allow her to lead the siege at Orléans. Her mission was to help drive out the English during the Hundred Years' War and allow the Dauphin Charles to be crowned King of France.

Jeanne became the French mascot, despite never actually fighting herself or using her sword; holding her famous banner that bore the name of Mary the Mother, she represented the courage of the Holy Warrior, savior to the French nation, and claimed the title of "Maid of Orléans."

The king lost interest in her after he gained his crown, and she was captured by the Burgundians and convicted of heresy and witchcraft. But those charges were not the ultimate reason for her execution; she was actually condemned on the grounds of her perpetual insistence in wearing male clothing. Her unwavering conviction to dress how she wanted was what she was truly murdered for. At the age of nineteen, Jeanne was burnt to death at the stake. Her last words as she was dying were, *"Jesus, Jesus, Jesus,"* a spine-chilling last testament to her extraordinary faith in a time of what must have been unspeakable fear.

After her violent death, she quickly became recognized as a prophetess and messenger of God. In 1920, she was canonized by the Catholic Church. Jeanne's youth and innocence, yet overwhelming strength and courage, have made her a legend and an example of martyrdom and the power of spiritual faith. Her lesson and message is simply that in total surrender to that sacred place of faith and trust, one will find their courage and strength to achieve the impossible and the seemingly insurmountable. Jeanne d'Arc is the quintessential heroine and an embodiment of feminine intuitive wisdom, courage, and devotion.

JEANNE'S
PRAYER AND MESSAGE

My dearest one, please breathe in deeply and allow yourself to exhale all your worries and stress. Courage for what lies ahead—for the mountain before us that we must climb—is found in our faith. Faith is that mysterious and unconquerable belief that you feel in your heart; it is the knowing that you are connected to something larger than you feel. Strength is found within this faith and allows for you to embrace and embody courage. Courage is moving forward, even when we feel fearful. Courage, faith, and strength allow you to walk your path and know that you are supported on your journey. Let me hold your hand as you move towards your challenges and fears, with your head held high, in perfect knowing that all is well.

JEANNE'S LESSON

Jeanne's confidence, unshakable faith, and focus not only captured the imaginations and hearts of people in France, but it also riled and disturbed the patriarchal authorities of the time.

This kind of strength is rare, and seen in only a small portion of people throughout history; she serves as an example of ultimate courage, faith, and strength. Jeanne's lesson is to teach you how to find this type of courage. This kind of bravery comes only through a deep, profound faith.

What is courage? Courage is the ability to move towards challenges and fears, to face them head-on and climb the terrifying, metaphoric mountain ahead of us.

Fear is a familiar guest in our lives. It comes uninvited and can paralyze us like nothing else. Fear can stagnate our lives, hold us hostage, and stunt our growth and freedom. Fear can keep us small, stand in the doorway of our dreams and desires, and strategically block us from seeing our fullest potential.

So where does fear come from, if we didn't invite it in? Where does it reside? Fear is, as many spiritual sages have taught us, the opposite to love. To be at the other end of the spectrum from love must mean that it is *disconnected* from love.

Love is Source, and we are all *cups full of Source.* Just as we have unconsciously become disconnected from our own *cup full of Source*—our life line—so have we become disconnected from our source of Love.

When we are connected to Source through our hearts in an act of faith, we can feel the love and support from the energy of who we truly are and where we come from. When we are unknowingly separated from Source, we have forgotten to connect with our hearts and those in Spirit who guide us. This creates fear, allowing it to walk straight through the front door of your life, crash the party, and hijack you.

The truth is that fear is the belief that you are not taken care of, that you are not supported, and that you cannot make it. Fear forces you to believe that you are not worthy of something. Fear makes you believe you lack what is needed within you to move forward and achieve something dear. When faced with this emotional bully, one must ask themselves, *"What is it that fear is making me believe I do not have within my eternal spirit, and what is it trying to persuade me to believe I can't have?"*

Over the years, I have experienced the most crippling fears imaginable—fears that literally left me feeling hopeless and terrified at what seemed insurmountable challenges ahead. Fear could creep in anywhere, at any time, but most often in the middle of the night. Sleepless nights of worst-case scenarios, dire consequences, and unimaginable worries would plague me for years when I first became a single mother. Most of the time, none of these fears were logical, or even real, but fear has a wonderful talent of appearing authentic.

So how do we *find* courage? Where does it come from, and how can we access it? Jeanne speaks of finding faith first. Now, by faith, she means belief as opposed to religion, although it seems that having a religion does help somewhat in forming faith.

If you are not religious, you may have a spiritual understanding and connect with your spiritual nature and those who support you in Spirit. Faith is like a muscle: the more it is used, the stronger it becomes. Faith is a belief, an unshakable conviction, a confidence in something greater than yourself.

Faith isn't just about believing in a God, Goddess, Angels, or a passed love one; it has to come from within first. To always reach outside of yourself for spiritual support is only half the picture. If we don't recognize, understand, and truly integrate the knowledge that we are expressions of Source, then we won't be able to access the inner strength that is needed to conjure up courage based on faith. We end up just dismissing our own power.

In our heart—our *cup full of Source*—we will find our truth; listening to our heart never steers us wrong. In order to find the type of unshakable confidence Jeanne possessed, we must return to our *cup full of Source*. We must remember again who we are, what we are, and why we are here. We did not incarnate into this life without the intention to make a difference; our lives are not meant to be meaningless. We came here to experience a bucket full of emotions and expressions of who we are and partake in experiences we could never have as a bodiless soul in Spirit. We came here to learn, to heal, and to love. We may well have chosen difficult challenges for ourselves for our growth and healing, but we would never set ourselves up on this earthly plane without support.

Circles of support in Spirit surround us all the time. Light beings, angelic energies, soul groups of passed loved ones, and ancestors and special guides we have traveled with for lifetimes are all present for every one of us on this physical journey. Our soul made its courageous choice to come here and be who we are incarnated into right now, knowing that every step of the way it would receive guidance from Spirit. To *not* reach out and connect with this ongoing infinite supply of support is like having your car break down on the highway and not bothering to call roadside assistance. Likewise, not tapping into your own personal power and belief in yourself is a betrayal to the essence of who you are.

Guidance can come to us via our intuition and our hearts as a knowing, a voice, a feeling, an image, or a gut response. Whichever way we perceive spiritual guidance, we will have an emotional response to it, which is always positive and empowering. This becomes your heart's truth. If it is not positive and empowering, then it is *not* guidance—it is *fear.*

Tapping into your heart's truth about any given situation will never steer you wrong. When we are faced with frightening challenges and mountains of worries, we only need to get centered in our hearts, connect consciously to our *cup full of Source,* and remember why we chose to come here. It is then that we find our nugget of faith.

We can feel that nugget of faith as a belief that we are taken care of, that all that is happening is meant for our growth, and that every moment is perfect for our highest potential. Each moment serves us over and over again towards our own expansion and growth.

The belief that we are connected to something vast and more powerful than ourselves, and the realization that we are part of that vast power, is *our* ultimate empowerment. It is then that we begin to cultivate and grow the seed of faith.

The more we believe, the bigger the faith seed grows and the more we have to hold on to. It is in this moment that we suddenly find ourselves with the courage to move forward. Without this faith, we are walking blindly in the dark.

Praying, meditating, connecting with yourself in nature, conversing with Spirit in your daily life, acknowledging your blessings, and being in gratitude for them is the way to cultivate and strengthen your faith. It is this spiritual practice that nurtures the seed of faith, creating the unshakable conviction that you are looked after. Here stands the banner of courage. Tightly holding on to this banner, you have all you need to move right through the fear.

Walking through the fear causes the fear to lose its power, and helps you begin to regain yours. Once you have made your way through the dark tunnel, you will find yourself in the light at the other end. The fear has left the building and you have achieved your medal of strength.

Strength comes from having faith, implementing courage, and facing the fear. Strength is endurance during a challenge. Strength is power over the lies of the mind.

Reconnecting yourself to Source is an act of self-love. Fear, for all its outrageous lies and assaults, can be one of our greatest catalysts to growth and healing if we take a higher perspective.

If it wasn't for fear, we wouldn't be given the opportunity to show how strong we really are. So next time fear comes barging through your door, instead of getting lost in the dark, search out and connect with your Source—call home, and find your faith. There lies your courage and strength; claim it, and move on to the next earthly experience.

Reflections

FOR JEANNE'S LESSON

These exercises can be done with a notebook and pen
when you have time to reflect.

- Think of a time when you were faced with strong fears. List them out. Did you manage to move through them? Write "yes" or "no" beside each one.

- As you recall these fears, ask yourself if they still hold power in your life now. Sometimes recurring fears crop up at different times in our lives. If you are still afraid of something, what is it, and what is the worst-case scenario you believe will happen?

- Remember a time when you faced a fear and walked through it. How did this make you feel? What is your perspective on it now?

- How strong is your faith? Spend some time evaluating if your faith is unshakable or if it is plagued by doubts. If you have doubts, ask yourself why.

- How often do you use this faith to help you through your day? In what kind of situations do you reach out for help or go inwards for guidance? Does connecting like this give you comfort?

- List as many occasions as you can remember when you received guidance from your intuition that helped you move forward.

- Start a conversation with Spirit in the days ahead with whoever you connect to most. Ask for help or thank them for small little blessings during the day. Reconnect to your Source through this conversation, meditation, or prayer. Notice how you feel after you have spent a few days connecting.

- Think of one thing in the days ahead that you have been fearful of doing, resisted, and worried about. Write it out and list the things that frighten you about it.

- In the days ahead, after you have spent time connecting to Source, find the courage to do that one fearful thing.

7

Miriam

The Prophetess

*Choosing Hope
and Finding Joy*

A BRIEF HISTORY OF
MIRIAM

Miriam (ancient Hebrew: *Mara*; Tiberian: *Miryām*) has several meanings—
"Bitterness," "Wished-for child," "Rebellion," "Strong Waters," and possibly
"Beloved," since some scholars believe the name is connected to *Merari*
(Egyptian). All of these meanings bear witness to Miriam's character and story,
including "bitterness," which does not necessarily denote grief, as some may
believe—the ancient Hebrews associated the "bitterness" with great strength.

She was the sister of Moses and Aaron and the sole person responsible for
the saving of Moses from certain death, and consequently the people of Israel.

At the age of seven, Miriam prophesied that her own mother, Yocheved,
would give birth to a son, and that this son—Moses—would lead and redeem
Israel out of slavery in the land of Egypt. Miriam and Yocheved were the
Hebrew midwives at the time, and when Pharaoh ordered that all firstborn
males be killed (which would have included Moses), this prophecy gave Miriam
and her family courage and faith to hide Moses in the bushes of the Nile. They
knew with faith that he would be found, rescued, and treasured by the Pharaoh's
daughter. Miriam was given the nickname "Puah" ("whisperer") after this,
because she was said to have "whispered" her prophecies.

Miriam's unflinching conviction that this future was destined allowed her
to both have and give eternal hope in the future of her seemingly doomed
people. Together with her brothers Moses and Aaron, she led the Jewish people
out of Egypt and the shackles of slavery and into the Promised Land—Israel.

Moses was the first teacher of the Torah, Aaron was the first high priest of
the Jewish people, and Miriam became leader and teacher of the women and
a source of strength and hope for them. It was through her leadership, intuitive
insight, and eternal hope that the women of Israel were able to move through
their despair, darkness, and fear of genocide into a place of hope, trust, and joy.
The presence of Miriam's famous "well of water"—which provided fresh water
and was said to make flowers bloom for the entire forty-year journey through
the arid desert—became symbolic of eternal life and hope.

Miriam is also known for her tambourine (an ancient frame drum called a
tof) and her beloved "Song of the Sea," which is sung at Passover to this day.
When Pharaoh's army pursued the Israelites into the desert, as the story goes,
the waters of the Red Sea miraculously parted and the Jewish people crossed
safely. Pharaoh attempted to follow, but the waters closed again upon him.

Miriam then instructed the women of Israel to take out their tambourines and chant in joy and praise: *"Sing to the Lord, for He has triumphed gloriously; horse and rider He has hurled into the sea"* (Exodus 15:21).

For the modern Jewish woman, Miriam the Prophetess is an example of strength, hope, joy, and faith; she has become the symbolic leader and mascot of Jewish sisterhood, women's communities, and circles around the globe.

MIRIAM'S
PRAYER AND MESSAGE

Breathe in deeply, and allow all worry to flow out of you on the exhale. You spend so much time worrying about what might happen, feeling trapped by your experiences and situations, feeling anxious about your seeming lack of control. The truth is that you have at your disposal a choice. You can reach into your hearts and access a connection to your higher self and to Spirit. It is in this heart space that you can experience hope. Hope is a choice—you actively and consciously choose to hold on to hope. This hope allows you to let go a little of the fear of darkness and to have some trust and expectation that you will reach the light. My gift now is to remind you that hope resides within you at all times—it is found in the same places as your desires, wishes, and aspirations. Hope is a space full of light, possibility, and overflowing with the expectation of joy. It is this joy and hope that I wish for you to choose now, and to know that darkness is but a temporary absence of light. The sun will always rise in the morning, as it will in your own life in Divine timing.

MIRIAM'S LESSON

Before the Israelites set off on their long and arduous journey through the desert, escaping slavery by the Egyptians, Miriam had told the women to bring their tofs (celebratory drums). The women were baffled that they would need an instrument of celebration during such a terrifying and exhausting exodus out of bondage. But Miriam was a prophetess. She knew that the outcome of this journey was going to be one of rejoicing, and she told her female followers to have hope and bring those drums along anyway. Miriam encouraged the women to trust her and have faith in the best outcome and focus on the celebration of victory and freedom.

Miriam's unflinching knowledge that having, focusing, and believing in hope was the key to bringing her people into victory and celebration. Allowing the women to fall into despair and doubt would have created disaster; the women provided moral support to the men as they fought and journeyed through the exodus. Bringing the drums of celebration with them, even though they had not yet *experienced* that joy, was instrumental in giving her followers hope.

Hope, as Miriam says, is found in your heart—your *cup full of Source*. Remember, we come from Source; therefore, joy and love is our natural vibration and our birthright. When we access our heart space and *cup full of Source*, we access our *truth*. In this truth lies our deepest and most precious desires, which hold the vibration for hope and joy.

I want to take you on a little creative visualization—a small journey into your imagination that will help you access this hope and joy:

Sit comfortably, close your eyes, and when you are ready, think for a minute of some of your most precious desires and intentions for yourself. Choose the most potent of your wishes and, with your eyes still closed, imagine you are experiencing this wish right now. Continue imagining that this wish is true, and allow yourself to experience it in all its entirety. Become aware of how you feel; notice where you are, what you are wearing, if there are other people involved and what they are saying. Listen for any sounds and aromas, savor all the sensory aspects of this imagined wish, and linger in this experience for at least three minutes. Before you open your eyes, ask yourself what emotion you feel when imagining the experience of your deepest desire. Now open your eyes.

The emotion you felt was likely one that resembled joy. Your desires and hopes make you joyful; they cannot help but do so.

You just partook in a very simple exercise that, if done regularly and for longer periods, would without a shadow of a doubt shift the vibration within and around you, bringing a version of that vibration and desire to reality in Divine timing.

This is how you intentionally co-create and manifest: actively being in the vibration of that which you desire and using your natural-born gift of imagination to take yourself out of the present reality and into your desired reality. In doing so, you hold hands with the universe and *create* that which you desire. The more you do it, the longer you do it, and the more detail you put into it, the more you shift the vibration you are holding to one that matches your desired outcome.

The more you give yourself the opportunity to experience the feeling of joy, the more joy is able to show up in your life. Intimately spending time with your hopes allows you access to your joy. This is a fundamental law of the universe; if you can learn and master it, this law will allow you to become a purposeful creator.

Miriam's lesson is that in times of darkness and hopelessness, you must remember that *you have a choice.* Your choices are either hope or doubt. By choosing to hope for a better outcome, you can allow yourself to imagine and feel that positive outcome and in turn experience the joy it brings. In doing so, you shift your energy and frequency from defeat to victory, dark to light, hopelessness to hope, and from disbelief to belief.

At any given moment, you can choose to have hope and experience joy in this way. Most of us tend to choose doubt and fear, however; many of us do this because we are frightened of disappointing ourselves or having too bold an expectation. It is true that rigid expectations can set us up for disappointment, but that generally occurs when we have forgotten to hold the vibration of our desires. Miriam's lesson teaches us an act of self-love, which allows us to choose how we want to feel, what we want to experience, and to fly with a higher vibrational feeling, rather than drowning in a frequency of doubt.

How much better would we sleep at night if we choose to do that simple visualization technique and focus on our hopes, rather than on our long list of worries and fears? Remembering who we are—*cups full of Source*—enables us to remember that we are here to experience whatever we wish, whether light or dark, but in that freedom of will we can choose to experience our hopes, too.

Disciplining ourselves to hold the frequency of hope and joy is an act of self-love. It simply gives us access to our natural state of being and opens the door to creating a life filled with our dreams, wishes, and aspirations.

Reflections
FOR MIRIAM'S LESSON

These exercises can be done with a notebook and pen
when you time to reflect.

- Think of a time in your life when you chose to worry endlessly and sit in a place of doubt and fear. You may have done this *many* times. Try to remember if, at any time, the worrying and doubt actually helped or served you. Did the worry or doubt influence your life in any way? Did it affect your health?

- Where did you learn to worry? Where does your habit of doubt stem from? Did you hear your parents worry all the time as you were growing up? If so, what was their dialogue? Does it match your dialogue now?

- Think of times in your life when you chose to be positive, to search for hope and focus on the desired result. If you can remember such times, what happened in the conclusion of those events? Did they work out for the best? How did that make you feel?

- Think of both the positive/optimistic and negative/pessimistic people in your life. How do these individuals make you feel when you are around them?

- In the days ahead, practice the creative visualization technique in Miriam's Lesson. Start with just three minutes a day and increase as time goes on until you are able to hold that visualization for up to thirty minutes a day. Please don't think too much about your wishes coming into fruition in between the practices, however. Allow the universe to do the hard work and deliver you what you have created in its own time. Take a step out of the control room and just enjoy the process of experiencing within your most precious hopes and desires.

- In the coming weeks, be mindful of yourself when faced with a challenging situation. Sit with it in contemplation, take a deep breath, and ask yourself what is the best outcome that you want and need from this situation. Focus on that outcome, or do the visualization practice on it if you wish. Simply hold the best outcome in your heart and either ask for it, expect it, or even better: decide just this once *not to worry about it.* Decide not to be victim to your circumstances and the experiences that crop up in your life. Decide to simply hope for the best.

8

Guan Yin
MOTHER OF
COMPASSION AND MERCY

*Compassion and Forgiveness for
Others and the Self*

A BRIEF HISTORY OF
GUAN YIN

Guan Yin (Chinese variant forms: *Kuan Yin, Quan Yin*; Pinyin: *Guānyīn*; Sanskrit: *Avalokitasvara*) is short for *Guanshiyin,* meaning "observing the sounds of the world." It was said that Guan Yin heard the cries of suffering of all sentient beings in the world. In Chinese Buddhism, Guan Yin also means the "Bodhisattva Avalokiteshvara"—the enlightened personification of compassion and mercy. Originally, in ancient times, Guan Yin was depicted as a male Bodhisattva, but over the centuries it came to be understood that these "enlightened" ones could show themselves as both genders or any other form required to relieve the suffering in those they wished to comfort. Many believe Guan Yin is genderless, but she is often depicted as a female Goddess figure.

There are many stories and legends told about her origins, the most well-known being that of her as the young and pure Miao Shan, daughter of a cruel and punishing father. The most profound part of that legend was that she began her journey to heaven after suffering terrible torment and abuse by her father. After her death, Miao Shan was about to move into the spirit realms, but she heard the cries of the suffering from the world below and became Guan Yin. Full of compassion, mercy, and forgiveness, she chose to return to earth, vowing never to leave until all suffering had ended.

Guan Yin is the patroness of fisherman and seamen, and her energy is associated with the pink lotus, symbolizing purity, peace, and harmony. She is often depicted with a dragon (wisdom and power) or a dove (fecundity), with many heads and arms to help her in aiding so many. Most commonly, she is shown holding a small jar filled with the nectar of life, compassion, and wisdom to be sprinkled onto her devotees with the branch of willow leaves in her right hand. The willow branch is a symbol of flexibility whilst weeping.

Guan Yin has become one of the most beloved archetypes of the Mother Goddess Divine, a beautiful feminine energy who resides in and around us for all eternity.

GUAN YIN'S
PRAYER AND MESSAGE

Breathing slowly in and out, imagine your breath to be like the tide, ebbing and flowing on the shore. Life experiences will flow to you as if they are washed up on the shore of your day, some creating positive emotions, and others provoking negative ones like sadness, anger, and resentment. Our emotions also ebb and flow. It is important not to hold on to the ones that do not make us feel our natural state of joy and harmony. Your life is filled with a spectrum of experiences. As one experience washes in and out of your life, allow your heart to gently let go of it, and thank it for visiting you. Do not hold on to resentments, pain, hurt, or fear. Allow them to come as welcome visitors in this party of life and then allow them to leave gently, looking for the blessing and gift they have to teach you. Forgiveness is a surrendering of holding on to that difficult experience that has passed, that which has flowed back into the ocean of experience. Do not try to keep hold of it, for its time with you has gone. Forgiving yourself and others is vital for you to create stillness and peace in your heart. Be grateful for this experience, for it has bequeathed you a moment of growth. Release with forgiveness, so that you may be free to experience the blessings, joy, and other experiences wishing to flow to you.

Guan Yin's energy is on the same plane as Mother Mary's. When I painted Mary in 2013, I had Guan Yin with me the entire time. Both are energies in a dimension that hold the vibration of maternal love. Guan Yin is Mother of the East and Mary is Mother of the West.

Guan Yin's energy is incredibly serene and peaceful. There is a stillness to her vibration, and one feels a depth of wisdom and knowing in her presence. The feeling of compassion that emanates from her is emotionally overwhelming, and it is easy to find yourself surrendering, allowing her mercy and love to pour over you.

It's important to say before we talk further about the subject of forgiveness that for those who have experienced the pain of unspeakable physical or emotional abuse, neglect, or criminal misconduct in any way to themselves or a loved one, it is vital to point out the need for trauma release and healing. To embark on a path of self-love encompassing forgiveness and to not release trapped and embedded trauma within the body, mind, and spirit is truly setting oneself up for failure. Trauma release and healing is something that should be focused on first with a qualified and trained facilitator—note that the process for this can take weeks, months, or years. How each individual works through this process is highly individualized, but cannot be rushed or overlooked.

If you feel you fall into this category, I urge you to get the necessary help so that the trauma that inevitably will be lodged in your physical, emotional, and mental systems can be safely released and you achieve some satisfactory level of emotional freedom in order to move into and through this delicate and fundamental lesson and experience of forgiveness.

In this lesson, Guan Yin talks about forgiveness; its components are compassion and mercy, and the very act of forgiveness is one of the hardest for us mere mortals to undertake. When we think about having to forgive another who has hurt us, and to forgive ourselves for our own wrongdoings, we struggle with the very concept, sometimes for years and years. Why is it so difficult to forgive?

To forgive oneself or another, one must access compassion: one must see themselves or others as a soul struggling through the maze of life, missing the mark on occasions and sometimes steering far off course from our true nature.

When another has wronged and hurt us deeply, we often hold on to that story for the rest of our lives, struggling to let it go. We cling on to these events and experiences that have caused us pain and sadness, tell the story to others

to share our pain, and write the events into the story of our lives, defining who we are because of them.

For some, the hurt and trauma runs so deep that, as mentioned at the beginning of this lesson, the need for help in releasing it is imperative. For others, the resentments of the past tinge and flavor our lives, and we subconsciously hold on to them for longer than we need to. Is the need to hold on to our resentments a need to remain a victim? It is quite common for us to find comfort in victimhood, however repugnant that might sound to our rational mind. We believe we are right and the other is wrong, and we claim the *need* to be right as more important than letting go. For some, our hurts are so deep, our sense of control shaken, and our anger remains unsoothed by the deep need to be right or to have our hurts witnessed. For some, our sense of self has been violated and the wounds are deeply embedded in our system. We want to let go, but we feel imprisoned by the pain we feel when we remember the experience. We continue holding on to the injustice in order to feel justified. Does our need to be justified in an experience with another who has done us wrong prevent us from seeing their soul and the others' suffering? Does holding on stop us from accessing our true, compassionate nature and keep us locked in bitterness?

We know that we have come here to experience different emotions and circumstances for our growth and healing. When tackling the aspect of forgiveness, we must always be mindful that we choose and create our own experiences. We set them up so that those very experiences can teach us more about our "self." For some, this is a very hard concept to take on, particularly if we have suffered abuse as an innocent child. It is important to remember, however, that our souls are steering the ship, and all that comes our way is for our soul's growth and benefit. This is a spiritual truth, and it is damaging and false to believe we are random leaves blowing around in the winds of life; we are all here for a purpose, and that purpose is to grow through our experiences. Our souls choose these experiences, however disturbing they may have been.

Holding on to experiences that have caused us so much pain is counterintuitive. Why would we punish ourselves with this stubborn resistance?

Guan Yin is the Goddess of Mercy and Compassion; we need to tap into compassion to enable ourselves to forgive. It is impossible to feel forgiveness without accessing compassion. Compassion is a form of love and empathy for another's situation or emotion.

When we look at those who have hurt, betrayed, abandoned, abused, or rejected us, Guan Yin teaches us that there are two types of scenarios that unfold in life.

The first is that of a person who commits terrible crimes against another, such as rape, murder, abuse, stealing, or some other violation. It is easy to feel hatred and disdain for this person, and our pain sometimes makes us want to hurt them, too, so we can relieve ourselves of our own pain.

However, when we look upon the individual who has committed these violations, we must nevertheless acknowledge that they are a soul just like us. To think otherwise would be a lie. They too are a soul in a body having a life experience, and they too have their own *cup full of Source*.

They are sentient beings whose souls set themselves up with certain scenarios so that they can play out roles that benefit themselves and others in one way or another, just like our souls did for us. Some souls choose to come here and play at being lost in the dark, and some choose to be examples of the Light. *All* of us have free will and *all* of us are connected with each other, helping one another to access more of our true "self."

Knowing that we are all *cups full of Source*, we understand that we are *all* pure Light energy coming from a Source of love. When we witness someone doing terrible wrongs to another, we have to notice the glaringly obvious disconnection from their Source. To be that unconscious about one's actions against another human being clearly indicates that they are unconsciously disconnected from their true nature. Just as we can easily choose to feel hate towards another, appalled at their actions and their lack of light and love, so can we easily choose to remember who they really are and feel empathy for their disconnected state. Hatred, after all, is yet another form of disconnection from Source.

In this acknowledgment, we can feel compassion, put ourselves in their shoes, and imagine how it must feel to be so unplugged from our origin. We can ask ourselves how difficult it must be to feel such a hardening of the heart, to be so disengaged with the roots of who we are. There is a dark emptiness within this condition, and if we allow ourselves, we can empathize with the other who is trapped in it.

In this understanding lies the compassion. Please let me clarify that there is no requirement to love or even like the other, but the emotion of compassion softens the resentment that can be all-consuming. There is no condoning the bad behavior or forgetting that which has been done to you, but deep in our compassion is forgiveness, and this is our key to our freedom from this past experience.

The second scenario is that of someone who is following the directions of their own heart, and thus going somewhere *we* do not want them to go. Many times, we are hurt by another because they have decided to make choices for themselves that we disapprove of. Family members, spouses, friends, and work colleagues may choose what they believe is right for them, but it doesn't sit well with us. Some examples might be:

- A child that tells their parents they are gay, leaving the parents filled with anger, hurt, and resentment because the child is not fulfilling their life the way the parents desire.
- A man that marries a woman outside of his religion, leaving the parents bereft and unforgiving.
- A daughter who cannot accept her father, alone and lonely, coupling up with a woman she does not approve of.
- A wife who leaves her husband because she has fallen out of love with him and found love with another.

These are but *some* of the examples of ways in which another hurts us—not because they are *disconnected* from their Source, but because they are very *connected* to their Source and following their hearts.

Holding resentment towards another because they didn't give us what we wanted is a common occurrence; yet how much pain do we cause ourselves and others when we cannot accept that we alone—and not any other person, regardless of relationship—are responsible for our happiness?

Being true to ourselves and following the guidance of our own hearts and souls is our given right, even if it upsets the apple cart. Therefore, accepting that we personally would want that freedom to follow our own hearts helps us to allow others their own freedoms.

We may feel loss and grief at the outcome of another's choice, but to hold resentment towards them is futile and misplaced. The more we can access our empathy and compassion, the more our resentment begins to shallow. It lessens the grip of anger, and our hurt towards the other softens because we see the truth in the situation and acknowledge that we are all sacred *cups full of Source*.

As Guan Yin teaches, experiences and people come and go. If we keep holding on to those people and situations from our past, we have no room left for all the new, beautiful experiences and people waiting to flow into our lives. If we don't look for the blessings, lessons, and growth, we can get stuck in our own prison of bitterness. Guan Yin talks about experiences flowing in and out of our lives, like the ebb and flow of the tide on the shore.

Use this knowledge in a creative visualization to bring peace to your soul:

Take a moment, close your eyes, and imagine that now all these different experiences, people, emotions, and chapters in your life are all washing in and flowing out with the tide when they are done.

Asking yourself what kind of scenario your resentment is locked into will help you understand which kind of person your "perpetrator" is: Could it be one who has lost all connection to the truth of who they are, causing harm and hurt to another because of it? Or is it one who is following the guidance of their own heart and moving in a direction opposite to what you desire for them?

When working on forgiveness, it is imperative to remember that in most scenarios we never will receive an apology from the other. Waiting for an apology to open the door to forgiveness is dangerous, because we put our own freedom on hold. Apologies may never come and the other may never be able to have the insight or awareness that they require to understand the damage their actions may have caused. If you are blessed enough to receive an apology, then accept it with grace and gratitude. But if not, don't waste your precious time being enslaved by your own resentment. See the *truth* in the experience and *let it go.*

The feeling of true forgiveness is such a beautiful surrender. It is as if all the cells, muscles, tissues, organs, and joints in our body breathe out a huge exhale. Forgiveness is truly a release from the grip of an experience that has passed. Forgiveness says:

I allow you to be who you are, exactly where you are, and to believe what you believe. I acknowledge you as a soul just like myself, and understand that what you have done towards me has no bearing on who I really am. My soul is much brighter than any hurt you may have caused me, and because of this, I have no need to hold on to it."

Forgiveness for others is an experience of freedom—a gift to give to yourself. It is an act of self-love to forgive others, and it is an even greater act of self-love to forgive ourselves. Each day we are a little wiser, a bit more savvy, awakened, aligned, and knowledgeable. Remember, we always have free will, and within this free will we can choose to remain stuck. In any given moment we are all doing the best we can with the knowledge and wisdom we have processed up until that point. However, we often chastise ourselves for things we would forgive easily in another. Self-love demands that you forgive yourself for not being perfect. It demands that you forgive yourself for missing the mark and for not knowing what you didn't know when you made your mistakes, but which you know now, having grown from them.

To ask another for forgiveness—yet not give it to yourself—is an act of self-harm. We have already learnt the lessons of unconditional love, self-honor, self-respect, self-worth, self-care, and self-comfort. How then can we not give *ourselves* the gift of release and freedom that is self-forgiveness? Our bodies, our aura, our very *vibration* resembles a dam opening in the instant we let go and forgive. The power of the release is unmistakable, and it is vital for your soul to grow, expand, thrive, and shine.

Forgiveness must be incorporated as a necessary act in our daily lives. Every day we make mistakes, each day we need to ask someone for forgiveness or apologize. Each day we are shown through all the myriad of experiences *more* of ourselves; each day we learn something new and evolve a little more. Each day we take one more step back to our *self.*

As ever, at the heart of it all remains our *cup full of Source,* which holds all of our light, love, and compassion. Spending time in this space allows us to see our fellow man, our greatest enemy, or our biggest perpetrator as just another soul, either living from their heart or not. How we choose to perceive them and our reactions to our experiences is what determines if we are free or living in bondage.

Reflections
FOR GUAN YIN'S LESSON

These exercises can be done with a notebook and pen
when you have time to reflect.

- Think of people in your life who you resist forgiving and are resentful towards. Make a list of each person, briefly describing why you resent them. If you discover you have more than four people on your list, this is a warning signal that you may have a pattern of holding on to resentment.

- For each person on the list, ask yourself, "Are they type A—a person who hurt me because at that time they were disconnected from their own heart and true nature? Or are they Type B—a person who hurt me because they were being true to themselves and they chose to do something that I didn't want or approve of?"
- Next to each name on the list, write why you feel they did what they did to you. Can you empathize with them now, even though they hurt you?
- In this understanding and empathy, can you look at them and see them as fellow souls and cups full of Source? Can you find compassion for them?
- Write a letter to each one, describing how you feel about what they did to you and expressing your new understanding of the situation. This will allow you to release your feelings of resentment. Burn the letters after, when you feel ready to let your truth go.
- Now, after finding some compassion for these fellow souls, are you able to release this experience? Can you see it flowing back into the ocean of life as the tide just carries it away, making space for new experiences to flow to you with a different vibration?
- When you finally begin to feel yourself releasing, you may need a good cry, sleep, a walk in nature, or a sea salt bath. Help your body release what you have been holding on to for so long, and be gentle with yourself.
- Now ask what you have yet not forgiven yourself for; find an understanding and empathy for it, and when you access that, gift yourself compassion and release.
- Say the Ho'oponopono: *"I am sorry, please forgive me, thank you, I love you."* This short but powerful Hawaiian mantra offers humility, apology, acknowledgment of the lesson learned, and recognition of the other's soul (or your own). Saying this mantra frequently and using it as a meditation helps shift your vibration out of resentment and into forgiveness and release.

9

Morgan Le Fey
THE WATER SPIRIT
*Embracing the
Light and Dark in Our Lives*

A BRIEF HISTORY OF
MORGAN LE FEY

Morgan le Fey, Morgana, Morgaine, Morganis, and Modron—a figure of deep mystery, confusion, and misrepresentation, Morgan has become such a profound, complex character that unraveling the truth of who she was and where she originated is now an incredibly difficult pursuit. A key figure in the Arthurian legends, her origins trace back to Druidic lore in the Celtic culture of the fifth century. An ancient pagan belief describes the Sisterhood of the Nine Morgens (Welsh/Breton: *Mari/Morgans*, meaning "water spirits").

These water spirits inhabited the mystical marshlands outside of Glastonbury; it was thought that moving through the "Veil"—the mysterious lakes shrouded in mist—would bring you to the magical, healing Isle of Apples—Avalon, the Otherworld.

Morgan le Fey was a healer, shape-shifter, and a faerie spirit who brought healing and prophesy to those that called upon her. Almost 700 years later, as Christianity took hold of pagan Britain, new literature was written on the mysterious, compelling stories of King Arthur and the various characters associated with him. As mentioned in chapter 2 on Guinevere, authors such as Geoffrey of Monmouth, Chrétien de Troyes, Sir Thomas Malory, and others each had their own version of this legend, twisting and changing the stories to such a degree that they sometimes left little resemblance to the original source.

Morgan has been depicted in some tales as a high priestess of Avalon, learning her skill of magic from the sorcerer Merlin; in other versions, she learned healing and magic as a child in a convent. As Christianity influenced people's beliefs, Morgan's magical and healing abilities were later expressed as dark sorcery, witchcraft, and evil. In some literature she is written as the nemesis of Arthur and Guinevere, the jealous victim of the unrequited love of Lancelot, and the mother of Mordred, whom she bore with her half-brother Arthur—and who later brought down the kingdom of Camelot. A myriad of versions of these stories are available, each contradicting the other.

She also is wrongly confused with Morrigan, the Irish Celtic Goddess of war and death. It is believed that the Church deliberately merged the stories of this Irish dark energy with Morgan's Welsh archetype, hence reinforcing the belief that magic, healing, and mystery are evil and the work of the devil. Celtic scholars are now clear that these two feminine archetypes are *not* connected, though it is true that they share the symbolism of the Raven. Morgan's association with the Raven, however, may be understood as the ability to shape-shift, hold mystical wisdom, and connect to the Otherworld beyond the Veil.

The many versions of Morgan bring to our attention the play of light and dark, good and evil, healing and destruction. In the powerful paradox that she has become, we must remember her origins as a gentle water spirit of the deep mystery, an illusive elemental of the natural world, a Goddess, and a priestess of the highest honor in a pagan/Druidic land that revered the balance of the God/Goddess of Nature.

MORGAN'S
PRAYER AND MESSAGE

Take a deep breath into your body and exhale slowly through your mouth. In your stillness, I ask you to imagine the aspects of light and dark, black and white, good and evil. You will realize they are extreme polarities of each other, yet you will find them at the ends of the same measuring stick. In the mystery of life, there is not just one side or the other. There is not just the dark and the light. There are in fact myriads of hues and tones in between that make up the deep mystery between this world and the other. In your search for answers in the magic behind the Veil and through the mists of time and space, you will come to journey through all of the hues and shades of life. You will experience the light and joyous all the way to the dark and sorrowful. This is where the magic lies, and this is where your soul asks to experience the mystery in all its wisdom. Embrace all aspects of your life, your personality, and your experiences. Try not to see them as black or white, right or wrong, but to experience them as stepping-stones of different colors and shades of reality, enriching your experiences here and creating a tapestry of magical ingredients to become more of who you are.

In and around our world we are inundated with news and media that consistently bombard us with images and stories of darkness. Crimes, murders, terrorism, unspeakable violence, and webs of corruption flood our news channels daily. Watching the news has become destructive to our mental health, and our constant connection to social media has made it feel that we cannot escape the perceived darkness that constantly surrounds us.

Amidst this darkness we are horrified, repelled, heartbroken, and feel heavy with hopelessness. In our hopelessness we can only feel empathy for the victims and disdain for the perpetrators. Mostly, we sit helpless in a place of fear.

At any given time, however, we can choose to switch the news *off,* disconnect from social media, and focus our attention on that which gives us pleasure. We can take the experience of the fearful news, use it to access more love within ourselves, and focus on sharing that love with others.

Ironically, the dark and negative events of our world are closely and sometimes intimately related to the light and positive events around us. Often, extreme acts of love and compassion are witnessed amidst tragedy and sorrow. The negative and the positive are strange but intimate bedfellows; *both* are customary and expected flavors of life.

The same happens in our own personal lives. Some days we experience joy, ease, light, peace, and contentment; other days, nothing goes right, life is a struggle, and we are heavy with burdens.

Most of us at some point will experience a trauma: loss of a loved one, job, or security; depression; illness; abuse; or something else that brings darkness to our lives.

We label these experiences as "dark times," and most of us would do anything to avoid them. All of us would rather experience peace and quiet, joy and happiness. Life, however, is not made up of only rainbows and unicorns. The wheel of life makes its turns whether we like it or not, and accepting that we are going to experience something other than the best of our days at some point makes the transition in our lives from light to dark somewhat easier.

Too often we resist and fight against the "dark times," blocking or pushing them down so we don't have to experience or feel them. We dislike having to sit with feelings of grief, fear, or sadness, and we strive to fix those feelings, white-washing in a vain effort to escape them altogether.

When we have experienced a lot of darkness in our lives, we create a bank of negative experiences. This bank of darkness is rarely processed; piles and layers of unattended negative emotions and experiences sit and fester, collecting and accumulating in the cells, tissues, and organs of the body. But this is not the way. It is imperative to face and feel our emotions during dark times head-on; we must process and allow the emotions in their entirety to flow through the body. Resisting these unpleasant emotions does nothing to dispel them. The only way to move through a dark time is to walk through the experience. It is impossible to reach the end of a dark tunnel and find the light without walking through the tunnel itself.

Repeatedly refusing to acknowledge these negative experiences brings an unending, nagging depression and cry from our soul. Many people drown out the cries of their soul through addiction or substance abuse; others may acknowledge them but never process them, instead using these cries as stories to illustrate their lives, creating excuses for themselves and evoking sympathy. These individuals allow their negative experiences to define them as martyrs, remaining trapped in victimhood.

Within each challenging experience comes an opportunity for growth. We all know that what doesn't kill us makes us stronger, so we can see that each dark situation is a *gift* for us to find strength and courage. The dark times fortify us, testing our faith and endurance; they are a necessary part of our evolution, and without them we would stagnate and remain unevolved. Our souls crave and desire experiences of *all* kinds, not just the rosy ones. Our souls know that the tough experiences will help us shine brighter. After all, diamonds become shiny under pressure, and so do humans.

As we have discussed before, it is important to remember that there are no true victims or perpetrators. We set up our own experiences in order to give ourselves the lessons and opportunities our soul needs in this lifetime. Nothing is given to us by our higher self that we are not able to handle, and, as we have learned, forgiveness allows us to live an emotionally, physically, and mentally free life.

Morgan tells us that good and evil, dark and light, negative and positive are on the same spectrum as each other—polar opposites, yet on the same plane.

Darkness is an absence of Light. In the presence of Light, we cannot have darkness. Imagine now yourself in a room with no light. In the pitch black of darkness you strike a match, which gives you a small token of light. Use that match to light a couple of candles and you have a little more light. Bring in a few more candles and there's even more light. With each candle lit we move out of darkness, but it takes many candles to shed enough light to eliminate all the shadows in the room.

Similarly, on a color paint scale from black to white, in order for the color to gradate to the white, we must go through more and more additions of white paint. Through all the many gradations of gray, each one gets a little lighter before reaching the full saturation of white.

If we use this paint scale as a means of illustrating the shades of our life, we can see that the "brightest white" kind of experiences are relatively rare. We may experience up to three days of the brightest white in our lives, but the rest of our lives are made up of all the hues in between. Likewise, it is rare for us to have more than three days of the blackest shade, and although we may have days dogged by depression or loss, they will likely match a darker gray day rather than our deepest, blackest day.

In between these two extremes are hundreds of gradations of mediocre days, joyful days, tired days, sad days, indifferent days, forgettable days, and pleasant days. Sometimes we may have a whole bucket full of shades of experiences in a single day. Excitement and optimism in the morning, disappointment and exhaustion in the evening. In essence, our lives are a myriad of shades of gray, with unpredictable bursts of white and black thrown in for good measure.

These shades of experiences make up and design the tapestry that is our lives, and in this, we can see the depths and perspective of our life's events. Our souls wanted to experience all the shades in between the dark and the light; only through those shades can our soul reach its own depths and perspectives. In this tapestry we find the experience of human existence.

Morgan's lesson is to accept and embrace all the shades of experiences in your life. When you give each one the same value, you reap and provide so much more meaning and richness to your own journey. The moment you can talk about the dark times and negative experiences with as much reverence and honor as you would discuss your wedding day or the birth of your child—extracting the lessons and blessings—you can remove yourself from being a victim of circumstance and understand that *you* are the creator of your own tapestry.

Just as our lives are painted in all shades and hues, so is humanity. No one can claim to be all light and love all of the time, just as no one can truly be filled with dark and hate constantly. We are all shades and hues of light and dark, and individually, some days we may feel lighter than the next. Some days we also show our darkness, which is in all of us. Our shadows come from our own bright light and cannot be ignored, dismissed, or feared. As we embrace our darkest of experiences, we must do the same for our own dark expressions.

Integrating and being compassionate towards all the shades of ourselves is an act of self-love. It is impossible to love one's self fully and completely if we do not love our underbelly, also.

Reflections
FOR MORGAN'S LESSON

These exercises can be done with a notebook and pen
when you have time to reflect.

- List three joyful, light-filled experiences that stand out in your memory as being the most positive, happy moments of your life.

- List three dark, sad, sorrow-filled experiences that stand out in your memory as being the most negative moments in your life.

- Write the blessing and the lesson that you received from each of these experiences.

- Contemplating your life, notice in your memory the ordinary days when not much happens, when there's no big drama and you are just living your life and getting things done. Understand that these days are just as valid and important as the lighter or darker days.

- List three of your most positive aspects and three of your most negative aspects. It is likely you are proud of your positive aspects, but ashamed of your negative ones. Try to access your compassion for the negative aspects, allow understanding for them and where they come from, and embrace and love these aspects as you would your own child. Offer forgiveness for each of the dark aspects within yourself.

- List three people in your life who you admire and three people you dislike, and the reasons you feel this way for each set.

- Look deep within and search to see whether you hold any aspects within yourself that are similar to those you dislike in another. Now allow yourself to forgive those aspects within yourself and in the people you dislike.

10

Artemis

MAIDEN OF THE HUNT

*Independence, Boundaries,
and Focused Intention*

A BRIEF HISTORY OF
ARTEMIS

Artemis (Greek, derived from *Artemes*, meaning "healthy and vigorous") was an ancient Greek Olympian Goddess, whose Roman equivalent was Diana. Her origins appear to be pre-Olympian, possibly even pre-historic, and she is linked with the Ephesian Artemis, who was a nature and fertility deity.

The Artemis we know today, however, is firmly placed as the daughter of Zeus and his mistress, Leto. According to legend, Leto gave birth to twins, Artemis and Apollo. Artemis was born first, and whilst Leto was in terrible pain delivering Apollo, she came to her mother's aid, actually acting as a midwife for her brother's birth.

As a young child, Artemis was very focused and headstrong, knowing what she did and did not want in her life. She asked for permission to remain an unmarried virgin and to become a huntress with bow and arrow. She wished to have maiden nymphs and hound dogs who would act as her constant companions and protectors. Five stags pulled her chariot, and she lived amongst the plains, marshlands, forests, and mountains of the land. The Cypress tree was sacred to her, as was the amaranth flower.

One of the many myths about Artemis is that of her one true love, the giant hunter Orion. Whilst showing off her hunting skills to her brother, Apollo, she accidentally shot and killed Orion with her arrow. In deep sorrow and grief, she placed him amongst the stars, now known to us as the Orion Constellation.

There are many stories of Artemis's bravery, clear decisiveness, and deep connection to love of nature and wild animals. Apollo and Artemis were known as both protective and destructive Gods. In one moment they could inflict disease and suffering and, in another, offer great healing and protection. Just as Apollo's realm was that of protector of young boys, Artemis was the protector of young girls, especially those unmarried or in need of help during childbirth.

Artemis was associated with the new moon and the evening, and thus she is often referred to as the "Bringer of Light." Fiercely independent, she teaches women to become self-sufficient, face their fears, seek out their goals, and never be constrained by the expectations of culture and society. It is not surprising that she has become a role model, archetype, and beacon of Light to women's rights activists around the world and women searching for their own inner strength, focus, and empowerment.

ARTEMIS'S
PRAYER AND MESSAGE

Be still, be quiet, and bring your attention to the rhythm of your breath. When we are still, we become independent of what is going on around us. When we are wrapped up in our outside reality, we become dependent on that which is not part of ourselves. When we are quiet, we can listen properly to the whispers of our soul. Bringing yourself back to your breath—finding your center—allows you to recalibrate and align with what it is you wish to do next, finding autonomy inside, which then allows for one to become master of one's self. Having your body, mind, and soul all in alignment with each other enables you to become self-sufficient and powerful in your intentions. When you are not aligned in this way, you will miss your mark. To become a master co-creator, you need to take the time to find your balance. Each part of your being needs to be vibrating in the same frequency so that all of your being is behind your intentions and choices in this life. Being determined is only a partial component to using the power that you contain. Finding the time and space to create alignment with all aspects of yourself is the key to hitting your target. Finding wholeness and oneness in yourself in this way means that there is no need for you to depend on others to create the life you want. There is no value in being fragmented in your energy; this will only bring a reality that is not fully realized. Finding balance in your life—meditating, being quiet in nature, becoming still, just being, rather than always doing—this is what allows for secure footing and self-reliance, and ensures precise focus.

The word "independence" conjures up the idea of being self-sufficient, self-supporting, and self-reliant. For some women, this idea may fuel the fires of empowerment within; for others, it may be a goal they haven't yet reached, but like the sound of. Artemis was the epitome of the independent woman in striving to live her life on her own terms, despite the demands of her culture. The true root of being independent is *not* being dependent on anything or anyone, and being in complete control of your own experience.

When society speaks of independent women, this usually refers to women being self-sufficient, women who live without a man by their side. This indeed was correct for Artemis, but it also means being independent of other's beliefs, choices, and dogma. A woman who can be socially, financially, and physically independent of another is one achievement, but to be a woman who has mastered a level of detachment that allows her to become *master of the self* is another. Being completely self-determining of one's emotions and vibration is another level of independence that we can all strive for.

Where is it appropriate in our lives to be dependent on another, and where do we need to become more independent? Certainly, there are times in our lives when we need to depend on another, such as illness, trauma, or loss. Relying on the help of another is a healthy practice, because as we learned from Mother Mary, reaching out for help and support is both necessary and nurturing.

However, as we grow into adulthood our emotional health can become deeply entrenched and contingent on another's, and this is where we can get into trouble. The majority of people are brought up being codependent. Parents teach it to their children, and both become entangled in a web of codependency, which is then repeated in relationships and generations down the line. Codependency is like an addiction. Its grip over logical thinking and rational decisions can leave you feeling powerless in its intensity.

Relying on another's reactions, choices, and actions, and being dependent on them for one's own state of happiness, security, and worth, is the very core of codependency. If you do not heal yourself from this addiction, it will trap you and cripple your life.

It takes an enormous amount of strength and courage to break free from the addiction of codependency, the roots of which come from a lack of self-love, self-esteem, and self-worth. It is one of the healthiest things you can do for yourself. Our goal is to achieve a level of self-worth and be independent of others for our own happiness, which of course brings us back to our own infinite supply of unconditional love—our *cup full of Source*. It is in connecting back with the self that one finds all that one needs.

Being responsible for the frequency of one's own vibration is imperative to achieving independence. If we give someone else the power to determine our mood, beliefs, and actions, we hand over the keys of our life to another. It is never someone else's responsibility to make you happy, and if you believe it is, you will find yourself on a long road to unhappiness and disappointment.

It is only *you* who gets to determine the vibration that you broadcast to the world. Only *you* can shift it and raise it by the quality of your thoughts and beliefs. Once you understand this concept, you are on your way to emotional freedom.

The opposite of codependency is inter-dependence, which is when both people are responsible solely for their own emotional well-being and both are vibrating at a level of wholeness and self-reliance. When two people achieve this and come together from this perspective, they are able to dance and flow to the rhythm of their relationship with mutual equality and empowerment.

Artemis talks of being still—that is, quieting one's mind and body to reach a place of complete stillness and alignment. Artemis suggests this is the correct state to become independent of everything around you. This independence of outside reality is a state of detachment wherein you disconnect from that which is not your true self; in this state, you mentally, physically, and emotionally become autonomous within. Detachment (or non-attachment) from what is going on around you allows you to see with clarity the truth of any situation.

Artemis recommends bringing all fragments of yourself back into alignment and finding time to focus on yourself to achieve balance and oneness. This can only be done by meditation, regardless of how that may look for you—sitting still and focusing on your breath; contemplating the stillness of a lake; or being lost in the rhythm of gardening, walking, or knitting. There are hundreds of ways to meditate, and no one way is the right way, so you must do what feels right in your own heart. No matter how you meditate, in being lost to the outside world, you will realize that *this* is where you find your true self.

Whatever transports you from your outer world and brings you back to your inner world is a form of meditation. When we can disconnect and detach from all that is going on around us and focus in on our own self, then we are connected in a place where we can meet the fullness of our soul.

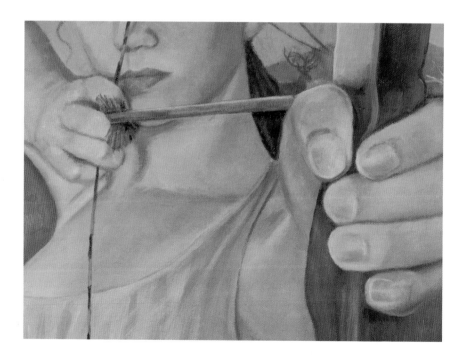

A person who loves to cook may be in her zone for hours undisturbed in the kitchen, deep in her joy, connected to all of herself. Likewise, another can swim laps for an hour and be totally unaware of the other swimmers around her, because in this rhythm she is connected to who she really is. Meditation can be staring into the mystery of a candle's flame, or it can be a solitary hike up a mountain. The meditation is what brings you to yourself, but in that connection there is a requirement to find stillness within, which can magnetize all the fragments of yourself back to its source.

When we are brought back to wholeness in this kind of practice, we can access our actions and goals with a focused intention. If we try to act and achieve from an uncentered space, we lessen the power behind hitting our target. Mastership requires steady footing, and meditation back into your center enables you to find this solid foundation.

It is an act of self-love to take the time to come home to yourself, finding your own self-governance, and becoming your own master. In this alignment, there lies our greatest power.

Reflections
FOR ARTEMIS'S LESSON

These exercises can be done with a notebook and pen
when you have time to reflect.

- List three things that you enjoy doing that bring you into meditative stillness inside. What can you do that gives you the centered harmony to feel at home within yourself?

- In the coming days, intend and commit to doing at least *one* of these meditative practices, and be sure to do it no less than three times a week.

- Alone in this quiet space, imagine that you have scattered and fragmented aspects of yourself as you have gone through your days. Imagine now that you can bring them back to yourself with your intention. See them fitting back together again inside, as though you are a broken mirror and all the pieces are magically being restored to wholeness.

- From this whole, empowered center, practice visualizing and focusing in on your goals and intentions, as you learned in Miriam's lesson (chapter 7).

- Reflecting on your life, notice those whom you may be codependent with. Is it your parents, your children, your partner, or friend? How does this codependency make you feel? Who in your life may be codependent on *you*, and how does that make you feel?

- Where in your life can you achieve more independence, so that you do not rely on another so much for your emotional well-being?

- Now think of a time in your life when you had to depend on another. Depending on others is sometimes imperative for survival, and for the one supporting you, many times it is a karmic debt. If there is any shame around this dependency, give it your unconditional love and compassion. If it is ongoing and needs to continue, allow it to do so with gratitude.

- Imagine and visualize your most important relationships in a dynamic of inter-dependency, where both people are independent and self-reliant within themselves and come together with you in an empowered relation of mutual wholeness and respected boundaries. How do you feel in this new dynamic of "inter-dependency?"

11

Kali Ma

THE
DARK MOTHER

Endings, Beginnings, Allowing for Change

Kali Ma (Sanskrit: *Kālikā*, or *Maa Kali*, meaning "darkness" or "beyond time") is normally depicted as the most ferocious and fearsome of all Hindu deities, yet she is revered and adored more than all the others. As her name suggests, she is the energy of pure creation, destruction, and the darkness of nothingness from which she comes. It is within this dark nothingness that pure consciousness exists; here, both the destructive and nurturing aspects of creation and life are born.

Conflicting myths describe her origin, but the most popular is that she was born from the brow of the great Mother Goddess, Durga. Kali was the forceful offspring who would bring about the destruction of all that was false and the slaying of all that was ego-driven. She is often depicted in bloodthirsty scenarios and disturbing representations, which has, over time, made many fearful of her power. However, these frightening depictions are steeped in symbolism and speak of a much kinder, protective, and powerful energy. Kali's mudra (Hindu symbolic hand gesture) is of that blessed protection and her yantra (Tantric sacred symbol) contains the energy of all that she is.

Often Kali is represented with a string of fifty skulls around her neck; these represent the "Garland of Letters," each letter of the Devanagari alphabet (used in the writing of over 120 languages, including Sanskrit) holding a Divine wisdom and Divine energy. Kali represents all of the energies and wisdom of each Sanskrit sacred letter; hence she is often called the "Mother of Mantras."

Kali is always depicted as having blue or black skin, symbolizing her non-corporeal, unmanifested form—the force behind creation. She is ever-changing, has no permanent quality, and her expansiveness is within the darkness of the chaos and perfection of the universe.

Kali is pure Shakti (the feminine) and in Tantric traditions she is honored and perceived as the main consort to Shiva (the masculine). Their union brings about the Oneness, the completeness and merging of all aspects of the Divine and its universes.

These qualities of pure, magnificent Shakti energy are the force that destroys the old and brings in the new. Kali is change; she is the hurricane that brings destruction to allow new life to come forth. She is beyond time, the dark hole in the nothingness from which everything is born. Yet, in all of this chaos, she is fiercely protective and compassionate to those who are true to themselves and their own divinity. Kali destroys all that no longer serves and gives birth to the new reality—both in our lives and in the universe as a whole.

KALI MA'S
PRAYER AND MESSAGE

Take a big, deep breath, and then release. Your life can never remain as it is in one given moment. Life—existence—is always moving, constantly changing, forever evolving. There is no beginning and there is no end. There is only the consciousness of now. Your life is entwined in the spiral of creation. Your life is flowing along the river of all lives in perpetual movement forward. You have many births and deaths, your cells constantly dying and being renewed. Look into my eyes and see your past, your present, and your future, and know that you are in my constant motion of creative perfection. When change is needed, you must surrender yourself to the storm that will shake up your present reality. You are to surrender to the flow of the winds of change and allow yourselves to be protectively swept off your feet whilst the energy of creation wildly but carefully lands you exactly where you are needing to be. This calls for trust and faith; it calls for surrender and laying your ego down at your feet. Allowing for change means you accept the endings of the now and open for the potential of the future. As my winds will never cease to stop blowing, your lives will never cease to stop evolving. Stop holding on, and allow me to carry you through the eye of the storm ahead and take you to safe and new shores.

Kali's energy is not to be taken lightly. It is powerful and life-changing, yet her storm can bring untold and unimaginable blessings. Kali asks you to hold on tight, but to trust implicitly the ride you are about to take.

One of our biggest fears as humans is that of change. Humans like familiarity and the comforting feeling of safety and security that it brings. In chapter 3, we learned through Brighid that resisting change only affords us an unwelcome struggle of swimming upstream. Endings and beginnings are what life is made of; life is a continual forward motion of unending cycles of change. The energy of Kali can be much like a hurricane, bringing great chaos, disruption to the status quo, and destruction to all that no longer serves. With this hurricane, however, comes an elevation closer to our highest potential. Whether it be a death, divorce, loss of job or financial stability, Kali's darkness can provide us with a shift in our circumstances that, although it may feel scary and unnerving, sometimes even bringing us to our knees, always lands us in a place of profound growth and support for our next chapter.

Weathering the storm and waiting for the eye of the tornado to pass before surveying all that has been uprooted and turned upside down is the key to riding this wave of change. If you have experienced this kind of shake-up in your life, then you will remember the feelings of instability, loss, grief, relentless worry, and doubt over what comes next.

Kali speaks of surrendering in her prayer. As with the path of "least resistance" that Brighid recommends, Kali asks you to stop struggling against that which is moving and changing around you. She offers unconditional protection; working with her is an act of faith and trust.

How does this connect to self-love? Deep within the storm lies precious, glorious jewels of strength and wisdom. Seeking out these jewels embellishes you with gifts you could never imagine, nor will you ever forget. When you struggle and resist against that which is meant to be, you cheat yourself out of the blessings and gifts the hurricane brings. Within the whirlwind of energy swirling around you in times of change, there exists the opportunity to experience the contrast of security. This gift of understanding the fear of the unknown allows you to create and access within yourself feelings of security and safety. Without this opportunity of contrast, we would not be able to access the desire for security within ourselves. Dramatic change enables us to find ourselves on a new and more fertile plane. As humans, we would never choose to cause upheaval in our comfortable lives, but the universe and our souls know that we need to be pushed into the storm to test our wings and encourage us to fly. Kali is tough love embodied; her love is uncomfortable, yet indisputably merciful and compassionate. Kali never wants you to get too comfortable. She is the catalyst for driving the creative, life-changing force of energy through you and your life so that you are ever-growing, ever-evolving, and ever-blossoming.

Once we have ridden the wave of change out of the storm, we see how much stronger we have become through the experience. As we have evolved, strengthened, and grown, we hold more Light within ourselves and shine brighter because of it.

When we come to accept and allow the notion that nothing stands still, nothing is permanent, and everything is always changing, then we will perceive our relationships, jobs, homes, and money in a new, enlightened way.

Once we realize that everything in our lives is there to serve our own growth, we can allow that which is all around us to freely perform its spiral dance. The only constant and unchanging aspect to all of this is our *cup full of Source*; this is our lifeline with unending support. Everything else is fluid, constantly moving and changing.

As with all endings, there are always new beginnings. As with all deaths, there are always new births. As one chapter ends, another is waiting to begin. When you walk this path in this knowing, you free yourself from anguish and suffering. Grieving is vital, but remaining victim to the storm and not going in search of those precious jewels is an act of self-harm. Self-love asks you to accept everything that occurs in your life with the trust and knowledge that it is for growth towards your highest potential. Our souls have a plan for us, and if we don't go willingly towards this plan, life will force us towards it, kicking and screaming if need be.

Kali wishes to empower you, not to beat you down. Your own free will determines how you ride the storms of your life. As a woman on the path back towards self-love, surrendering and remaining centered through the storm of change gifts you with unexpected reserves of strength and emotional maturity.

Asking ourselves the question when we find ourselves in the eye of a storm *"What must end to allow the new to be born?"* is vital. Sometimes, we know what needs to end, but we just didn't have the courage to end it ourselves. Other times, we only see the truth and wisdom of an ending when we have moved on and look back over our shoulders with a detached curiosity. Saving yourself from suffering and resentment by surrendering to the endings and beginnings of your life is a precious, compassionate act of self-love.

Reflections
FOR KALI'MA'S LESSON

These exercises can be done with a notebook and pen
when you have time to reflect.

- Can you remember a time when vast change, upheaval, and uncertainty descended on your life? If the answer is yes, can you see it as a journey with a beginning, middle, and an end? Do you notice any difference between how you were at the beginning and how you were at end of that journey?

- What was your biggest fear during this upheaval and change? Did this fear come to pass? What lessons and wisdom did this experience present to you? During this experience, did you resist it at any time, and if so, did that make things harder for you?

- What did you need to understand that you did not comprehend before this experience? What needed to end that was not serving you anymore?

- If the experience was a deep loss, what were you meant to experience in this loss so you could find something else? What were you being asked to let go of so you could claim more of yourself?

- From your new perspective, are you able to sit in gratitude for this experience and journey?

12

STAR OF HEAVEN AND EARTH

*Disrobing of the False Self and
Embracing Your Sexuality
and Sensuality*

A BRIEF HISTORY OF
INANNA

Inanna (Sumerian: *Nin-an-ak*, "Lady of Heaven")—the exalted, ancient Sumerian Goddess of love, war, sexuality, and fertility. The Akkadians—the first ancient Semitic civilization of Mesopotamia four thousand years ago (modern day Iraq)—called her Ištar, meaning "Goddess of the Sky." Her famous temple in the city of Uruk was called the "House of Heaven." Inanna was connected with Venus, the planet/star seen rising in the east in the morning and descending into the darkness of the west at night. The great Babylonian, Phoenician, and Greek Goddesses Ishtar, Astarte, and Aphrodite are all latter names and incarnations of Inanna.

Associated with protection in battle, war, fertility, and prosperity, Inanna was also the embodiment of the potency of feminine beauty, love, and sacred sexuality. In her temples in ancient Sumeria, the *Hieros Gamos* ("sacred marriage," a sacred sexual ritual) was performed regularly, believing that the dark energy of war, destruction, and the anger of warriors returning from battle could be drawn out of the man and healed by the female priestesses of Inanna. This sacred marriage of sexuality was also thought to give legitimacy to kings and to fertilize their lands. This power to their throne was highly sought after, since they could not receive it otherwise. Hence, the power of this sacred ritual of Inanna was *immense,* and we have seen this ritual played out in many subsequent pagan cultures of old.

Amongst her many myths and stories, the most well known and reconstructed is that of her descent into the underworld. Within the many versions of this epic story, we see the basic underlying theme of descending into the depths of darkness/hell. Her journey is a symbolic descent into the subconscious and shadowy parts of ourselves. Inanna had to pass through the seven gates of hell, disrobing of her crown, jewels, and all aspects of her material power. The metaphor is clear: discarding the ego, shedding the superficial skin, and the death of all that is inauthentic. At the end of her journey through these seven stages of descent, Inanna dies; her resurrection and rebirth takes place three days later. Transformed and ascended as the bright star of the sky, she is now the light and beauty of the heavens and crowned the "Queen of Heaven and Earth." We can see clearly how the patriarchal religions later borrowed from this concept, and how many other Sacred Feminine archetypes were also given the same title.

Her symbols include that of the eight-pointed star and the looped reed stalk, denoting protection, fertility, and divinity, and later seen to influence the ankh and Isis knot of ancient Egypt. She is often depicted riding on the back of two lionesses and associated with the ancient and primordial bird and snake Goddess, with the wings of divinity and wisdom and the power, regeneration, and transformative healing of the serpent.

Inanna represents the independent, forthright woman who is strong and secure in her feminine sexuality and beauty, rebirthing in her constant cycle of growth, living in the light of her authenticity, and embracing her shadows and darkness.

INANNA'S
PRAYER AND MESSAGE

Breathe in, and allow yourself to relax on the exhale. Each time you exhale you allow a little more of what does not serve you to leave your body. When you are born, you are pure and whole, glorious in your nakedness, true to the divinity that you have been born of. All through your lives you pick up, take on, and embody emotions, thought patterns, and belief systems that do not belong to you. You wear these false energetic clothes as if they are part of you and yet none of them truly are.

As you journey and travel through your life, more and more of these false energetic clothes are put upon you, or even in some cases are chosen to be worn by you because you believe yourself to need them. There are many walking around cloaked in a disguise that they are completely unaware of. There are many who have no idea who they truly are and what they truly look like without these borrowed perspectives. It takes courage to unclothe yourself of that which does not belong to you. It takes authenticity and honesty to disrobe yourself of all falsehoods, beliefs, and behavioral patterns that do not mirror the pure light and magnificence that you truly are.

In your nakedness, in your deepest vulnerability, you will find your truth. Your beauty, sensuality, sexuality, your strength, wisdom, and dignity come from allowing yourself to be disrobed of all that is not you and to be seen and witnessed in your true bright Light.

INANNA'S LESSON

As we move through our lives, we pick up and absorb beliefs and habits that are either taught to us by others or claimed by us along the way for one reason and another. The majority of this happens during childhood; our parents and teachers instill in us what we then carry as our truth into adulthood. Inanna calls these "false energetic clothes." We wear these belief systems like garments and the frequency of them shapes our lives.

In the present, we can look at ourselves and see how we have created a version of ourselves wearing another's clothes. If we can dissect all of our beliefs about both ourselves and others, we can lay them out and recall who, where, and when we picked these up from. Our parents taught us what they knew, and as we know it is difficult to teach another what we have yet to learn ourselves. Having forgiveness for those who shaped our early lives is just as important as being honest in declaring where our beliefs come from.

Inanna talks of disrobing yourself from all inauthenticity. In the honest act of laying out your beliefs and thought processes, you can undress yourself from all that is covering up the authentic you. It can be an uncomfortable and unnerving process to work through, because at some point you will have to address the fact that a large portion of what has caused much of your suffering has been your own false belief systems gathered and knitted together from others to form your inauthentic clothing.

Examples of these false beliefs can be anything: a parent never praising you, so you believed you were never enough; feeling less physically perfect than your classmates, causing shame; feeling powerless when you were bullied at school; believing you are not smart enough because a teacher said you would never succeed; or feeling physically imperfect because someone decades ago laughed and mocked you in public. There is a myriad of negative beliefs that we could have inherited, absorbed, picked up, or claimed over the years. And though they were never true and never ours, nevertheless we have allowed them to define us.

When our natural creativity as a young child is neither encouraged nor praised, we tend to grow up believing ourselves to be less creative and inspiring than others. When we were never told that we were loved growing up, we believe ourselves to be unlovable. When our sexuality is abused, we believe ourselves to be sexually powerless. Taking the time to do this very important, deep self-analysis is imperative to a healthy mind, body, and spirit. Stripping ourselves of all that is not ours and disclaiming all that belongs to another is the core work of self-love.

As well as these false clothes, we also have our false ego. Egos rarely tell us the truth, and they are nearly always irrational and illogical. Our egos can be full of fear, jealousy, insecurity, and pride. The ego programs you to feel emotions that keep you small and trip you up. The ego doesn't believe in your *cup full of Source*; the ego believes you are lacking and in need. The ego believes you are never enough.

As mentioned in chapter 10 with Kali, in life there comes a time when we are thrown into darkness. We are forced by life into the darkness of our own subconscious through illness or traumatic events. It is here we are made to see our own shadows, and as Morgan le Fey teaches us in chapter 9, these shadows are equally important as our light.

As we make our own descent into our subconscious, we are asked to strip ourselves from all that is not the truth. In our pure nakedness that we were born into, we can rebirth ourselves as the authentic Light beings in a human body that we truly are. We can finally start living as *cups full of Source.*

When we stop wearing the ill-fitting, borrowed clothes of false truths, we are finally able to see our full potential, which is unlimited. There is no limit to our own magnificence. We are made of Source energy; finally seeing ourselves as such is not only exhilarating and freeing, but it is also our launch pad into our highest destiny.

As women, the ability to express ourselves emotionally and lay ourselves bare to another comes more easily than it does for men. However, as women, to physically lay ourselves bare is much more complex. It is not exactly news that women have major issues with their body image; how women feel about their own bodies is a topic discussed and analyzed to death. Most women will agree that they have—to one degree or another—body shame.

The female body has many functions. From being the vessel to hold and nurture a life, to being subjects of art and visual beauty throughout the centuries, and the enticement and embellishment of selling commodities . . . the pressure on us to accept our bodies unconditionally is immense, yet how we perceive our bodies is incredibly important to our journey back towards self-love.

Many women find it hard to look at themselves in a full-length mirror naked. It's hard enough to catch a glimpse of ourselves in underwear in the changing rooms of our favorite clothing store, but to voluntarily stand stark naked in front of a mirror and take a good look at ourselves is challenging, to say the least.

The gentle falling back in love with the vessel that keeps you alive on this planet is a slow and steady process. For some, losing weight and eating healthy changes their perspective; for others, conquering an illness or disease and watching the body heal itself is the turning point. For many women, learning to love and accept their bodies comes with age and wisdom. Tied into all of this is a woman's sexuality and sensuality. A woman's body is innately sensual. All human bodies are to an extent, but women are gifted with shape and softness that makes it intrinsically so. Sensuality is a gift of the feminine; it is pleasure-inducing, inspiration for the senses, and a powerful, integral part of the human experience on earth.

We are sensual creatures, and yet we can also find sensuality in the colors, textures, and sounds all around us. Sensuality is everywhere, if we know what we are looking for. The sensual experience can be found in the food we eat, the sound of our voice, our words, and the way we move. Sensuality is an enjoyable expression of *all* the senses.

The power of a women's sensual potency is enormous. As women, we have the ability to access this potency and share it with whoever we wish. This is different from "sexiness"; being sexy is when another perceives us as sexually attractive. Sensuality, on the other hand, is a power emitted through all five senses to inspire others to feel their own sensuality. All women have this power, but many are either unaware of it or unpracticed in using it.

As we work on loving our bodies with gratitude and reverence, we also need to stoke the fires of our own sexuality, however dormant it has been. We have already mentioned how the ancient priestesses of Inanna used their sexuality in the *Hieros Gamos* to draw out the war within men returning from battle. The softness and sensual bodies of these priestesses soothed and humbly unraveled the men so tightly bound by the horrors of war. It was a sacred act of enlightenment, a merging of the feminine and masculine in Divine Presence.

Now, I am not suggesting that this is something you need to pursue; what I *am* suggesting is that you give heed to the power of your own sensuality and sexuality, understand the pleasure it can give another and—more importantly— how it can give you alone your *own* pleasure and access to a power you may not have felt you had before. Our sexual power as women is gifted to us by the feminine aspect of the Divine in order to empower and fulfill us, and inspire others. That does *not* mean we are up for the taking, but it *does* mean we need to understand and embrace the pleasure, comfort, and joy our sensuality offers. This kind of feminine power is to be given the deepest respect and honor; it is something a woman should cultivate, enrich, and hold sacred for those with whom she wishes to share it.

If you are single, then you need to begin pleasuring yourself and taking the time to investigate and discover the hidden gems of delight within your own body and sensuality. If you are in a healthy and loving relationship, then you need to share your sensuality with both yourself and your partner, experiencing the giving and receiving of lovemaking that is open to you. Sensual physical pleasure is not the same as ordinary sex. Sensual physical pleasure is taking time to honor the body in oneself and another, extracting high vibrations of physical joy, love, and erotic sensations in a safe, loving environment. When this aspect of our self is healthy—even if we are single—we become fully integrated in the wholeness of who we are, and as women we embody more of the glorious Sacred Feminine of which we are all beautiful expressions.

These exercises can be done with a notebook and pen
when you have time to reflect.

- Make a list of the beliefs about yourself that you carry within. Here are a few questions to ask yourself: Do you believe that you are lovable? Do you believe that you are worthy of great respect and admiration from others? How do you feel about your body? Do you believe yourself to be beautiful? Do you believe yourself to be intelligent? Do you believe yourself to be talented? Do you believe that you are able to achieve great success? What are your beliefs about money? Do you believe you are able to achieve financial security?

- Now list a few of your beliefs about other people. Ask yourself the following: How do you feel about people from other races, countries, and religions? How do you feel about successful people? How do you feel about people who have a lot of money? What do you believe about people who are poor?

- Ask yourself if this is *your* truth—or did someone else impress it upon you? Did you absorb these beliefs from another, or are they your own in the present moment?

- Reflect on times when your ego may have gotten the better of you. When did jealousy, pride, and fear stop you from seeing your own Light?

- How do you feel about your own sexuality and sensuality? Do you feel you access and embrace it comfortably and easily, or does it make you feel uncomfortable and uneasy? If so, why do you think this is?

- Your sensual sexuality has much power. Used correctly, it can shift your life and vibration. In the days ahead and when you feel ready, find some alone time to give yourself the gift of self-pleasure. If you feel uncomfortable with this idea, be gentle with yourself and know that you may need to work on this issue more than most. If possible, create a space for yourself with soft music, a candle—whatever sets the mood for you—and give yourself this time to explore your own body, to gently caress that which is yours and that which is sacred to you. Offer yourself tenderness and unconditional love in this practice. The more you can give yourself the practice of self-pleasure, the more your sacral chakra will activate. The sacral chakra is the second chakra of our energy centers; when it is healthy and clear, it is very powerful in moving and shifting energy in both your body and your life.

- If you have a partner, work up slowly to sharing your body with them after you have had some time to give pleasure to yourself and see how much of a difference this makes to your love-making. Be mindful of your own sensuality, and become aware of how this opens up your partner's.

- When you are ready in the days ahead, take the brave action of standing in front of the mirror naked. Start slowly and with compassion for yourself, but make this a daily practice so that, in time, you can learn to love more the reflection in the mirror of your true, physical nakedness.

13

Grandmother Spider

THE WEAVER

Becoming the Wise Woman,
Weaving the Web of Your Own Life

A BRIEF HISTORY OF
GRANDMOTHER SPIDER

Grandmother Spider (Spider Grandmother, Spider Woman, *Tse-che-nako, Sussistinako*) is known in the ancient folklore of multiple Native American societies as the creator of the world and the universe and intimately connected with the Goddess of Teotihuacan in Mexico.

For the many hundreds of Native American tribes, including the Cherokee, Hopi, Pueblo, Navajo, Lakota, Coos, Ojibwe, Zuni, and the Choctaw, there are several myths and stories about the Spider Old Woman (Navajo: *Na'ashjéii Asdzáá*) who created the sky, brought fire to the people, and created the four races of humans. She molded out of clay the red, yellow, white, and black races, connecting each one with a thread from her web at the top of their heads (crown chakra) as a reminder that all are connected to the central Source via the web of life.

One of the most popular and well-known stories about Grandmother Spider describes her singing and spinning her web of creation. After she had embellished the strands of her web with dew drops, she threw this web into the sky, and the dew drops became the stars and planets.

The stories of Grandmother Spider are symbolic of the feminine aspect of the Creator. In the oral tradition of Native Americans, stories to explain the mystery and magic of the universe were passed down among the Elders from one generation to another. They understood and connected deeply with nature and the earth, and Grandmother Spider's web of creation helped them comprehend that everything and everyone is connected to this web of life.

Within each of these tribes there is a common honoring of the deep sacredness of both women and the feminine aspect of the earth and creation. To this day, we refer to the earth as "Mother Earth," and to nature as "Mother Nature."

Out of the dark, out of the void, Grandmother Spider, through her thoughts, dreams, and desires, weaved the web of life. The web is the matrix of the cosmos, the complex pattern of threads connecting everything to everyone. The spiral dance of the weaver is the spiral dance of creation. Grandmother Spider not only asks us to remember how fragile the threads are, but that we ourselves are these threads; whether we understand it or not, whether we believe it or not, we are all connected intricately and intimately to each other.

GRANDMOTHER SPIDER'S
PRAYER AND MESSAGE

Take a few moments to look at your life from a higher perspective—a more detached, less emotional viewpoint of the map of your life so far. You will notice that the paths you have walked on have taken many twists and turns. One path would branch into another, each taking you forward and back towards yourself. When you think of all the paths you have walked, you're reminded of the people you've met along the way, those who have come in and out of your lives to help you become more of who you are. Every person, place, situation—every opportunity and emotion you've lived through—has been created by you in partnership with the universal creative force in order to serve you. Everything in your life is beautifully connected to the other: to what came before, and what comes after. Everything you've experienced is part of the intricate web of your life. Each step is just one of the many stepping-stones along the way.

With your desires, dreams, intentions, thoughts, and beliefs, you weave your life into form. Everything is connected; nothing is separate, no one is alone. Everything is a thread within the vast web and matrix of creation. In each moment you are given the generous and unconditionally loving gift of creating what you desire. Each moment asks you to weave your most precious intentions into each breath you take so that you can experience in the physical that which will allow you to reach your highest potential. Creating a life you desire is an art form which can be mastered when you realize you are the creator.

So here we are at the very final chapter and lesson of this book. It could not be more perfect that Grandmother Spider wrapped up this series of paintings and collection of lessons.

Grandmother Spider is the creator of the web of life. She is the potent, magical aspect of bringing thought into matter and desire into form. She is the weaver, the cosmos, the universe, and this earth we live on is *her* manifestation. Grandmother Spider asks us to witness this outside of ourselves, but also *within* ourselves. She asks us to acknowledge the web of life we are part of and the web we also weave in our own lives.

When we look back on our journey, we may feel we have lived many different lives within our one life. The life you lived as a child may feel a million miles away from the life you live now. We can look back and see how different a person we were ten years ago to the person who is now reading this book. For some, it doesn't always follow that our circumstances improve through each chapter of our lives, and many of us may feel we are worse off now than we were five, ten, or twenty years ago. However, as we have learned, our circumstances do come and go, our experiences flow in and out of our lives, and without any doubt, our own level of consciousness will have expanded because of this.

Wisdom grows through adversity, observation, adventures, encounters, and most of all gratitude for all that you have been through and experienced.

All of these experiences have led you to this point in time as you are reading this final chapter. Life is ever-moving, ever-changing, and ever-expanding, and each step along the way connects you to the one before it and the one after it. Without even being conscious of it, *we are weaving the web of our own lives.*

Every decision we have ever made, even the ones we deem wrong, have created a new branch of potential and a new path to journey along. Everyone we have met has, in some way large or small, shaped and infused our experience with their own individual flavors. Looking at our lives from this bird's-eye view allows us to connect the dots, process, and digest all that we have been through.

From this higher perspective we can see there was *never* a truly "wrong" decision. There is, in fact, no wrong move, because whether we took the long way around or the short cut, whether our experiences were positive or negative, we always ended up growing and expanding from that experience; we always received what we needed to know and learn at that point in time. All experiences

and encounters along the way have been *on purpose*, *with purpose*, and *for the purpose* of growing and expanding into our highest potential.

Grandmother Spider wants you to acknowledge and accept the knowledge that you are the creator of your own life; *you are your own creator*. Believing that, owning it, and literally standing in that power is the heart of this lesson. She asks you to consciously and carefully weave the web of your own life with purpose and desire.

Our dreams, desires, and wishes are here to help us expand. They are here to be the ingredients in the threads in our life's design.

Your desires are there to stimulate you to desire more, desire different, and desire higher. Your desires act as the catalysts to keep moving forward, expanding, and growing.

In chapter 7, Miriam gave you a beautiful, powerful, yet simple practice to help get these desires in motion. Through her creative visualization, she showed you the power of how to access your desires within yourself before they come into form. This is consciously weaving the web of your life.

We have learned that each one of us is a *cup full of Source* housed in a physical body. When we detach from another, we can see that everyone is just like us, another thread in the web of life. We can see that others are also souls like us, struggling, growing, and experiencing.

Grandmother Spider teaches that *everything* is connected—there are *no* accidents in this earthly life, just co-creative *synchronicity*. When we access the understanding that we are all *cups full of Source* and that we all come from the same place, made up of the same Light, then we can access the One Consciousness and see ourselves as a unified collective.

It is always your choice how you live your life. You have free will to weave your future from the threads of your past, or you have free will to weave your future from the understanding of the present moment. None of us need to be defined or designed from the experiences of the past. All of our pasts can be gratefully let go; we have in each present moment the opportunity to create something new.

Grandmother Spider asks you to consciously weave your web from a place of clarity, detachment, gratitude, and unconditional love for the self. When these aspects are the force behind an intention, then your life cannot help but be designed and weaved with magical intent. What you weave will affect the lives of others because of our universal connection, and so with every new choice and decision you take, make it from your heart space; that way it will always speak your truth and affect others from a place of *love*.

FOR GRANDMOTHER SPIDER'S LESSON

These exercises can be done with a notebook and pen
when you have time to reflect.

- Take some time to sit quietly. Imagine yourself as an eagle, taking a literal "bird's-eye view" of your life. Try to see your whole life up until the present day from a higher perspective. Draw a simple map of the major happenings and stages from your childhood, to adolescence, through your twenties, and to your present age. Use dates, if you wish, and arrows to show yourself how one event or encounter led to another. You will notice how each meeting with someone significant led you to the next place, person, or situation. See how the dots are joined with what came before and after and notice how you weaved the web of your own life.

- In taking this higher perspective of your life, notice how you have grown in consciousness, wisdom, and in heart. Consider now where you may have taken the long way around with something and not learned the lessons you should have the first time. Were there any situations that repeated themselves as a result?

- In this present moment, you get to consciously decide where you want to go next. You can now choose which direction you wish to walk towards—and choose what to avoid and the actions you will not take from this place of wisdom.

- Congratulate yourself for all that you have been through and survived. Give yourself compassion and forgiveness for not always having made the best of choices, and realize that no choice was ever truly the wrong choice. Each situation and experience gave you exactly what you needed to learn, grow, and expand at that time.

- Whatever your age or stage in life, the wisdom that you have gained just from getting to where you are now is priceless and invaluable. Completing this book and giving yourself the opportunity to love yourself completely is truly the most precious wisdom of all. *Now* is the time to weave your web with the magical wisdom, desires, dreams, and intentions of your heart.

IN CONCLUSION . . .

In this book we have been on a journey back
towards our true "self."

Guinevere
taught us how to honor ourselves and our own majesty,
and to teach others how to treat us.

The Magdalene
showed us how to live from a place of unconditional love
within the heart, the epitome of the Divine Feminine.

Brighid
illustrated to us how to move fluidly
through the spiral of life, offering no resistance and embracing
the creative feminine flow of life.

Isis
helped us see where to access our power and how
to shine in our own light.

Mother Mary
offered us support and comfort, and reminded us to be gentle
in the way we speak to ourselves.

Jeanne d'Arc
revealed how to find our strength through faith and courage.

Miriam
bequeathed us with a practice to tap into our hope, joy,
and deepest desires.

Guan Yin
reminded us that forgiveness is the key to personal freedom.

Morgan le Fey
encouraged us to embrace all the different shades
of experiences in our lives.

Artemis
explained how to detach and become independent within our
own center and in our own mastery.

Kali Ma
showed us that beginnings and endings are but part of life—
to embrace them brings blessings and to resist them causes struggle.

Inanna
stripped us bare of our false beliefs like the shed skin
of a serpent so that we could be reborn in our true authenticity.

Finally,
Grandmother Spider
offered us the knowledge that we are the power,
the force, and the co-creator to manifest the life we want,
acknowledging our *cup full of Source* and our deep,
profound connection with all that is.

My wish for you all is that throughout this book
you have seen yourself differently, that your perspective is higher,
and your heart is more full with the truth of who you really are.
Self-love should feel like the right next step now,
and with some patience, compassion, and time, you should be
on your way to living your life as the magnificent expressions
of the Sacred Feminine that you are.

British born and bred, Jo Jayson is a self-taught painter. She began her career as a muralist in London, Sydney, and New York. In 2008, she began expressing Divine Feminine energies into her own paintings, completing her much-loved Goddess Chakra series. In 2011, she unveiled the beginning of her Sacred Feminine series of paintings, unfolding a body of work that contained thirteen channeled feminine energies. Jo has emerged as an internationally acclaimed intuitive artist and spiritual teacher, helping women all over the world find empowerment, healing, and inspiration. She sells her paintings, prints, guidance cards, and meditation tools worldwide. Jo Jayson continues to channel the Divine into her paintings and regularly teaches self-healing workshops online and around the United States. For more information, visit: www.jojayson.com and info@jojayson.com.